S0-ABD-083

The American Poetry Series

Books by John Logan

Cycle for Mother Cabrini (1955)

Ghosts of the Heart (1960)

Spring of the Thief (1963)

The Zigzag Walk (1969)

The Anonymous Lover (1973)

The House That Jack Built (1974)

Poem in Progress (1975)

Only the Dreamer Can Change the Dream (1981)

The Bridge of Change: Poems 1974–1980 (1981)

Only
the Dreamer
Can Change
the Dream

Only the Dreamer Can Change the Dream

SELECTED POEMS

John Logan

The Ecco Press

NEW YORK

Copyright © 1955, 1960, 1961, 1962, 1963, 1964, 1965, 1966,
1967, 1968, 1969, 1970, 1973, 1981 by John Logan
All rights reserved
First published in 1981 by The Ecco Press,
1 West 30th Street, New York, N.Y. 10001
Published simultaneously in Canada by George J. McLeod, Ltd., Toronto
Printed in the United States of America
The Ecco Press logo by Ahmed Yacoubi
Typography by Cynthia Krupat
Library of Congress Cataloging in Publication Data
Logan, John, 1923–
Only the Dreamer Can Change the Dream: Selected Poems
(The American Poetry Series, 21)
PS3523.0344A17 1981 · 811'.54 80-23184
ISBN 0-912-94677-6 / ISBN 0-912-94678-4 (pbk.)

The epigraph by Rainer Maria Rilke on the dedication page
is taken from his "Letter" (1920), *Letters to Merline*, translated by
Violet M. MacDonald, London, 1952, pp. 47–49. Reprinted by
permission of Methuen & Company, Ltd. and Editions du Seuil.

Grateful acknowledgement is made to The University of Chicago Press for
permission to reprint the poems from *Ghosts of the Heart*, © 1960 by The
University of Chicago Press. All rights reserved. Grateful acknowledge-
ment is also made to E. P. Dutton Company, Inc. for permission to reprint
the poems from *The Zigzag Walk*, and to Liveright for permission to
reprint the poems from *The Anonymous Lover.*

*I would like to thank the John Simon Guggenheim Memorial Foundation
and the Research Foundation of the State University of New York for
grants which made completion of this book possible. —J. L.*

For Guenevere
For the children—now beautifully grown men and women—
And for the new grandchildren

All that the rest forget in order to make their life
possible, we are always bent on discovering, on magni-
fying even; it is we who are the real awakeners of
our monsters, to which we are not hostile enough to
become their conquerors; for in a certain sense we
are at one with them; it is they, the monsters, that
hold the surplus strength which is indispensable
to those that must surpass themselves. Unless one
assigns to the act of victory a mysterious and far
deeper meaning, it is not for us to consider ourselves
the tamers of our internal lions. But suddenly we
feel ourselves walking beside them, as in a Triumph,
without being able to remember the exact moment
when this inconceivable reconciliation took place
(bridge barely curved that connects the terrible with
the tender . . .).

—Rainer Maria Rilke

Contents

Spring of the Thief (1963)

The Zigzag Walk (1969)

The Anonymous Lover (1973)

Cycle for Mother Cabrini

[1 9 5 5]

Pagan Saturday

Hiking out to Ratcliff
School we took our shoes off
In the field of stubble
Where the graveyard ends; we ran
Shouting thru the stalks

Of pain that grow tipped
And colorful as grain.
We swarmed the woods and looked
For fun and fuel and packed enough
To pile and build to a roar

A very satisfying fire.
We set our mouths on hopes
Of stolen corn and raided
An easy field behind a barn;
And burst the milky kernels

On our thumbs. Letting
The fire at one side turn
To ash we buried our yellow
Catch inside its wraps of husk
And later, ate in heights

Of joy the cindered ears.
Then racing along the rim
Of Indian Gully sudden
As fear light as laughter I felt
A creature flare with beauty

At the back of my eye;
I knew my limbs and body
Sang on me sometimes—

But this was brighter than my arms.
Coming back we played

Some rapid hide-and-seek
Among the graves; I hid
Awhile and searched the stone
Face for Mother; and ran on
Into the pointed groves of pine.

A Dialogue with La Mettrie

Since thought visibly develops with our organs,
why should not the matter of which they are
composed be susceptible of remorse also, when
once it has acquired, with time, the faculty of
feeling?
—La Mettrie, *Man a Machine* (Leyden, 1748)

Where does one look
To purify the remark of an ancient
Cynic? I am afraid not
To the eighteenth century
And the mechanist La Mettrie;
If he is one, for here
The ambiguity

Begins. Let me explain.
The ancient has us build on
Supposed Plato's supposed
Definition, Man is two-legged
And without any feathers: add,
To tell him from the plucked bird,
His nails are flat.

Now this idea of the dog
Diogenes shook me. But,
Let me say, no more so
Than the mind of La Mettrie.
I think we are not mushrooms
Swollen for a day, nor even
"Flowers bordering a ditch."

And I want a violent leap
Beyond the dog. Do not
Tell me from him as you mark

The ape by his more intelligent
Face. For once there was
A blurred and giddy light
In my enormous eyes.

A few more wheels a few
More springs than in,
Say, your better animal?
And with a closer heart
To fill the brain with blood
And start the delicate moral
Hum in the anxious matter.

Suppose I agree the soul is
An engine, admit Descartes
And the rest never saw
Their pair of things—never,
As you say, counted them;
Then here's the ambiguity,
And a further problem:

You say you find an inner
Force in bodies, and watch
The smallest fiber turn
Upon an inner rule.
Now I don't see that this
Is such a clear machine!
In fact I think I wish it were.

For I have weighed
Your evidence: I don't forget
Your newly dead
And opened criminal
Whose still hot heart
Beats like the muscles in the face
Of the severed head.

I don't forget you say
The flesh of bats
Palpitates in death,
And even more of snakes,
That never sweat. "Why then
Do men boast moral
Acts, that hang on these?"

Besides injected warm
Water animates the heart;
The hearts of frogs move
If put in the sun or if the heart
Is placed upon a hot
Table or a stone. If it stops,
It may be poked or bathed.

And Harvey noted this
In toads. (The great physician,
I could add, once
Professionally cut a toad
A burnt witch had kept
For her familiar,
And found it puffed with milk.)

A piece of a pigeon's heart,
Lord Boyle has shown, beats
As the whole one did.
It is these same motions
Twist along the eel,
In spiders or in the tiny
Hands sliced from moles.

And last, Bacon of Verulam
Has in his *Book of Spears*
The case of a traitor caught
And opened alive: his heart

In a pan of boiling water
Leaped several times
To a perpendicular

Height of two feet.
Let us then conclude
Boldly! Man is a machine.
And there is no other thing
Underneath. Except I believe
Ambiguity, with its hope
Or its ancient agony;

For to what do we look
To purify his remarks, or purge
His animal images? What
Piece in us may be cut free
Of the grieved matter of La Mettrie,
That underneath a temporal reeling
Took on this arch of feeling?

The Death of Southwell

A Verse Melodrama

with Homilies on Light and Sin

I never did take so weighty a man,
if he be rightly used.
—Richard Topcliffe, *Letter to the Queen,* July 6, 1592

Cold dawn Harrow-On-The-Hill.
The unquiet curtain is too
White this hour, the candles
Too drawn their flames rest-
Less ruddying the cup
Of thin breads with its thin
Hands not yet bodied
In the dawn: the priest's face
Floats like cloth fair
For sacrifice, watch! his vestments
Are gaudy as dawn light grows.

Topcliffe's horses shake
The steam of gray morning; men
Grow sad with cold.
The house is sketched well-marked
Where mass is said. What argument?
The traitor's vested. Take him.
Cloak his colors! These horses
Scream. Now load his books,
His papist images; and this
Damned altar furniture
That burnishes with sun!

Westminster six o'clock
Topcliffe binds him hangs

His hands to pull the gentle
Wrists with weight of flesh.
God its bulk on these thin bones!
Down from the altar to be tall's
A curse. How real these heavy
Limbs! Is death a stretching
That makes flesh more slight;
A thinning of the blooded brain?
And emptying of eyes.

Fainting breaks these days
And nights by the wall. Toes
Touch sometimes. Won't
Say priests or people or place
Of meeting or color of his horse
That might be seen by houses.
Fainting breaks it. Look!
Here's fire! The child flames
In white and wintered places!
The paper lit to his face
He vomits blood, and wakes:

"Your fire is angular as pain and keen
As stone that killed the haunted Stephen.
Still its corners cannot hide
Its numbers or its god. Why look these gentle
Fires gesture to their home. They're tongues
Of doves are leaves and many-colored prongs
Of bush. How can a Child of Light
Forget His every perfect gift
Of art or ken! Well then! Our Christ
Is our Prometheus: His steep
And formal angle keeps our flame!"

No mass how is a man
A priest, without his folk.

Why, when you come for cauliflower
Take away his blessing from his tower.
A poet and no ink? Let him read,
His Bernard's here; his Bible: the lilies
Business, foxes light
And blood of grapes the seven
Porches on the graying pool.
But he writes with pins only tallies
Of his sins and the pious name of Christ.

This priest that hath a boyish
Look's a man most lewd
And dangerous! Keep him closed
Three years lonely in his cell.
(Perhaps Arundel's dog shall
Visit him to seek the blessing
Lions gain that with
Their paws have digged the graves
Of saints.) And now at sword's
Point drive the traitor
Forward to the bar for trial.

He knew he'd hang, and the rest.
He was always very white of face.
What falconry he had he
Put in poems. Uneasy in disguise.
No champion. In fact quite
Unfavorably compares to Campion.
A slight man, a poet pulled
Into the common prose of crowds
And guts. The comic Cinna screams.
Ignatius offers English wheat
The lion's head shall thrash for bread.

He speaks from his cart at Tyburn:
"When you are free of the whale's

Belly you cannot hope
To sit with Jonas in the shadow,
Except some envious worm
Gnaw apart the ivy's
Root. And should you move
From thorn or briar to the sweet
Odored cedar, your worm,
That cannot breed in you shall gnar
About and snap his teeth.

"Your proper devil all his imps
And instruments shall feed
Like storks upon the venomous
And evil acts of men.
And shall rejoice, if we
Amend, at men's calamity.
The delighted ravens fly
To the smelling corpse, but won't
Hunt the sound body;
So the wicked flock and stick
About us if we stink with sin,

"But if the healing soul
Slough from it this wanted
Flesh, it will abandon too
These hundred melancholy loves.
In winter when the vine is bare
Let the devils lie:
They shall be struck in April
When the flower starts, and at
The wild scent of virtue
Die like snakes
Beneath the blossom of the lime."

HANGMAN SITS IN TYBURN TREE
PREACHER SAYS HIS HOMILY

12 /

NOW HIS CART IS PULLED EMPTY
HANGMAN HANGED HIM AWKWARDLY
LOOK THE PREACHER'S HAND IS FREE
BLESSES HANGMAN BLESSES ME
HERE'S A FRIEND TO PULL THE KNEE
GHOST NOW LEAVES HIS YOUNG BODY
THIS POET SAINT WAS THIRTY-THREE
THE HANGMAN MOANS IN TYBURN TREE
NOW UNBLESS HANGMAN, UNBLESS ME.

Cycle for Mother Cabrini

I / A Chance Visit to Her Bones

I thank God Mother Cabrini's
Body is subject to laws
Of decay. To me it is
A disservice when flesh

Will not fall from bones
As God for His glory
Sometimes allows. I say this
For flesh is my failing:

That it shall fall is my
Salvation. That it shall not
Conquer is my blind hope.
That it shall rise again

Commanding, is my fear.
That it shall rise changed
Is my faith. I think
I can love this saint

Who built high schools
And whose bones I came upon
Today. I laugh a little
At the wax mask that smiles

Surely through her box of glass:
Artificial faces cannot
Frighten one who remembers
No face is real for long.

Blessed Mother Cabrini
Lives here her saint's life,

I said, she sees me all;
I only see her face

Mask, and see her habit
Given form by bones
Which carried about her flesh,
Gone now. The bones will rise

To carry changed flesh
And I may walk—I
Might walk with her!
Whom I seek to pray to

Some, and strain
To love. Moisten me
With dust from her bones.
I see their shape—help me

Love them help think of
Breast white doves that rise
Over earth-smelling fields.
Their wings tremble for her

Birth, as I wait: mine
Is a dry waiting.
Her mask stares, she
Stirs—ah

Her bones move *me!*

II / *Recollection*

1

I found your bones that lay
Off the highschool hallway

And drummed them with my need;
They rang and rose and hurried

Me. I bought and set
Your picture in my wallet
And chose a cheap ring,
A piece of junk but something

Your sisters sell; to me
Its feel and pull heavy
On my fingerbone wore
In for a time the terror

Of your delicate flesh, the scant
Weight within the fragrant
Bones that it seemed turned
To me as to the bright and unburned.

2

Blessed Mother I know
You met me once in Chicago.
I didn't go there
To hunt for saints (or anywhere):

You bowed and smiled at me
Out of a film biography.
I don't know why I went
Except perhaps for amusement

And rest; your skill is hid
Behind a sweet and lurid
Piety O queen
Of a Holy wood unseen—

Your eyes and art sent
A deep tiredness apparent

To me as an expected thing
But (until I knew) unsettling

Because of breathlessness
And a hot and blood shocked duress
At my ribs, that sickened me,
And turned the colors of the city.

3
Long years Mother had gone
Before I met you in Tryon
Park although you knew me
At Chicago and eternally.

One time in New York again
Under the wicked regimen
Of grace, I thought to come
To your girls' kingdom

To the middy world of your tomb
By text, principal, and schoolroom.
You know I did not go;
I went another place though:

Can I say what you did
Those days I invalid
At church, ambiguous at its door
Was tried by my confessor;

Without luster hair
Sprouts at arm's root bitter
Sediment upon the flesh dead
The nail slides from folded

Skin, so shall I be
Till Christ reafford the luxury

By which bodies sing
And souls have their breathing;

Sweet virgin it was you
That left the gay retinue
To cry me grace at its head
Till I like your bones was not dead.

4
Saint who overlaps
Our lives who knows the mishaps
Of our times the flaws
Of men no longer outlaws

Even; who knows our schools
Our stores our gods and business rules;
Who saw charts rise and fall
In your chromium hospital—

You helped shape our city
And the city in the sky:
Now help me shape your beauty
In this scarred and remade eye.

III / *Mother Cabrini Crosses the Andes*

1
The tiny saint got the best mule
Though an opera singer was in the party,
And St. Joseph the muleteer was gentle
And helped a lot; providentially,

For the soundest beast leads
And she had never ridden and was jittery—
Tried to guide! Though she learned
Early to be passive to the sea.

Small and weightless as she was
She could have risen to the saddle
Or St. Joseph would have tossed her
Humbly, could she have put

Her foot into his hand
But she could not, ascending
Rather from upon a chair
And set off cowled in furs

"Like a monk" (her saving comment)
Or Xavier in the mountains of the orient.

2

And the air in the high Andes
Was thin and lucid as milk
Or fire, or as violets she sailed
In boats in Lombardy,

A child afraid of the water
But sick for the fire and milk
Of the sea's wake and for the souls
That flashed like fish

For the souls that love like milk
And like fire, for the spring soul
That bursts quiet as a violet
And swings upon its thin

Stem to flame at the sun,
Ridiculous as a nun.

3

Had she known the pressure
Here will bleed the skin
Or that muleteers would be

Too busy to say the Rosary,
That she would fail to jump her mule a-

Cross a crevasse, would fall
Into St. Joseph's arms and
Faint in the snow bank that flanks
The rim (the heights of her cheeks
More pale more glowing than crystal
Vanishing on her habit—eyes

As they opened as soft as furs),
Or had she somehow discovered
She and Mother Chiara
Would spend the evening in a bar
Beside the pampas' edge: she

Would lead that pilgrimage again
Over the high Andes,
Forego the closed cabin,
The turn around the horn; would climb,
Would rest the party at the Cumbre
Again draw breath and for a moment again

Would turn away forever.

4
Air shivered in the Andes
As full of color as blood
Or bells, or ice the saboteurs
Left on Lytle Street
When angered by the sick and alien

They opened her mansion pipes;
Yet what was this to her
Who dynamites hearts: rivets,
Quarries, shapes bricks, and built

In Chicago two hospitals
Besides the one they chilled awhile

And burned a little bit.
But they kicked the sisters out
Of Nicaragua—the schoolgirls no trash
These, necks blue as Andes
Snow and thin as moons: hair

Black as the bird-live valleys;
The saint was away on business—
New Orleans orphanage or the villa
Or the novitiate at old Manresa
On the Hudson. (Or perhaps the hotel
In Seattle.) There was trouble in France

Since the archbishop was on the Riviera,
And the priests turned her a cold
Parisian shoulder, but she moved in
At a gilt estate where the sisters
Had to put up sheets over the many mirrors.

Whether they went on their continents
Or ours the austere skirts
Were strangest brushing by the summer-house
In Rio the intemperate flower parts:
Though here the black was closest
To the holy red that flowed her into God

In Chicago, upon her martyrdom.
She should have died in Lombardy
Safe from a saint's life and the traveler's
Malady that chilled her and brightened
Her gown, like a bell she jangled in her room
Where she rocked and, died, in a wicker chair.

5

A good mule like God's will and the sea
Does not mind those who disagree
And bore her safely
So that, the stars at easy
Height again, the party
Rested.

But the pampas at night are a sky
Where masses alive and unknown
Are relieved by constellations of bone.

6

High cold keen the Cumbre air
As the light from the stone and shattering stars
But there is nowhere mountain air
So cold or keen or bright or
Thin as is Francesca's wrist
Humming hyaline
Along the risen limb.

Ghosts
of the Heart

[1 9 6 0]

The Lives of the Poet

(T O W A L L A C E F O W L I E)

So much the worse for the wood that finds it's a violin
And to hell with the heedless . . .

Christ, éternel voleur des énergies.
—Rimbaud

1

His hour of birth he rolled
From his pillow to the
Floor having hoped a somewhat
Longer trip that day
Than this brief stay
From death. Although he fought
The usual Sunday walk
To church, Frederick and Arthur
Hand in hand, Vitalie
And Isabelle—each with a blue
Umbrella, Madame at her careful space:
Christ and thief to life.

2

He heard her shrill from the porch;
He flew to the farthest points
Of the garden wall and hid
His fists in his eyes
And felt the gate and fruit trees
Breathe, and discerned the envied
Inner lives of the vine.
Her shattering voice
Split the neighborhood games
And ruined the solitude even

In the latrine, where he tried fitful
Kinds of love and flight.

3

He traveled alone in his room
Lying on a canvas piece
Of sail harsh to skin
As salt burst to the novice
Lips or the pitch of deck
Underfoot. He found
The pilgrim roads of song
And played the keys of a book
In his lap; he carved the table's
Edge in the shape of a spinet:
But couldn't stand the braid and
Fat of the township band.

4

One day he left Madame
Waiting in a field;
And ran. "Come beloved soul
We *need* you," wrote Verlaine
(A view not shared at home) —
The boy had grown quite tall,
Sat ill at table; his peasant
Hands were huge and red
His hair and eyes unstyled;
He sneered at the talk and meal
And house and the pregnant wife, and fled
Insolently up to bed.

5

The white of the chair in his room!
The white of the stoned moon
Certain and alone, pearled
And unpassioned in its lights

Unhounded in the silence
Of its round O
Perfect sure voyager!
The white of the furniture the
Glow of the cube and sphere!
The joy and glow of the body
Of the boy in the cold window of his room
White or gold as the moon!

6

He saw in Verlaine a child
Of Sun—burnt by the ancient
Memory, moved on the ancient
Sunwarmed flank: struck
As the great brass bells
At the breasts of the cattle of the sun:
Pierced or wheeled by the sun-
Keen tips of the ancient horns.
But Verlaine, stuck by an ordinary
Arrow, moved with the faith
Of his fathers and made a minor sound
His Place and his Formula found.

7

Some are moved as the gray
Eyed Io by the god
From home and call: are hurried
To the drowsy lengths of the reed
Or the pulse of space to the west
Or east to the lands where huts
Of clay and wattles made
Are raised on wheels; where nomads
Turn with the feel of the goad—
Some have the face of a god
Some have the tooth of a swan, or the laughable
Lust-sad eye of the calf.

8

Always bent to depart (it seemed)
The poet took the Alps on foot
Suffered a stroke in the sun and was helped
By monks; was robbed on his way to Russia.
He caught a cold with a circus troupe
In the north. At last he joined the Dutch
And sailed to Java. He left and lived
With native tribes till he signed on His Majesty's
Ship. He hired on a farm in Egypt
And plundered a wreck in Suez and worked
As foreman in a quarry. He smuggled guns and slaves
And lost a leg in Harari.

9

He went home when hurt
And so his mother won
In the end. After the Verlaine
Melodrama he came,
His arm in a sling, and wrote
Une Saison en Enfer
In the barn (she heard him groan
And rave like some Saint
Anthony in his cave). She won
Too when he gave up his life
Of rigorous debauch and tried to help
Swell the family stock.

10

Madame and Isabelle together
Might be heard to cheer
When he thought of raising a child
An engineer. He gave up Verlaine
And the love of a native wench
And the gentle servant boy
Of Aden. Those fierce women

Nurse the men home
From the humid wars. They alone
Walked with him to his tomb
After Mass, they and he and the black trees
Shadowless in the rain-wet grass.

11

He tried in the bird the rule
Of the snow, the peculiar luck
Of flutes: so much the worse
For the boy who flies his home
And god and verse, for the brass
That wakes a horn. The weight
Of the gold about his waist
Shall make him sick. The horizon's
Shift of blue is a change
In the man. And the verse will clutch
And cast. And the apter alchemies
Of God make one change last.

After Fowlie and Aeschylus
and after a remark of Maritain's on Wilde

On the Death of
the Poet's Mother
Thirty-three Years Later

(TO ISABELLA GARDNER)

The tongue fits to the teeth and the palate by Number,
pouring forth letters and words.
—St. Augustine

Years ago I came to the conclusion that poetry too is
nothing but an oral outlet.
—A. A. Brill, M.D.

1

My mother died because
I lived or so
I always chose to believe.
At any rate I nursed
At a violent teat with the boys
Of the bronzed picture. In my
Memories of taste I find
Bits of the tart hairs
Of an Irish dog that hangs
Its red arch over me; I'm not
So sure of that beast
That it has stole as much from me
As I shall suck from it.

It had an eye of milky
Glass with a very
Reddened spot that sent
Threads or streams of red
About the eye's globe
And this eye moved
Among the long red hairs

At the skull of the dog as it
Leaped in the childhood grass,
As it springs in the childhood
Trace, as it arched and pulled
And arched and pulled the sheath of its livid
Tongue through the wisps of its breath.

July began with the Fourth
And the moon in a box
Like a flaming house in the grass
At the edge of the fair with the frames
Of the fireworks there, but next
It floats, like a carnival balloon
That drops out weights of men,
And turns the festival tips
Of the sparklers hot: fear
Shot up in a kite when it burned
My throat white—like an eye
My friend once cooked in his head, as he mixed
Carnivals of fluids in a shed.

Yet I was not so scared
Or scarred I could not
Scream and climb to find
My aunt to cry for help
High in the mounts of bleachers:
I saw a face and told it
All my needs, but my hot
Throat beat with fright
As a strange mother bent
From the stands—her flanks were blood
In the moon and festive light
As she heard my plea of hurt and
Saw my burnt neck twitch,

Arched over me a God-like Bitch.

2

Don't think I took this dog
Too quick for mother:
I looked for another in the book
Of art where I found the Latin
Kids at the dugs of the wolf,
But most of the stone women
Wore no clothes and some of them
(With help from a borrower's pen)
Showed the genitals of men.
I looked for her in girls
At games and aunts who said
Her face was mine—so I tried to catch
Her in some epicene line.

I guess I looked the most
In father's wife
Whose hair was Welsh and red
Who rocked me once so ten-
Derly on her lap
As I could not lace my boot
Today I remember that—
The boy and his mother and his shoe
His wrists so thin and his hands
Fit so wrong around
The square boot-thong the work
They did or sometimes would not do
Made him weep for them.

I looked in Palgrave's book
She left, and I looked
Through her pearled glass.
But did she read the verse?
And where in that still
Unpretentious town
Did turn the brass wheel

To clear the glass? How many times
I tried the German names!
And felt the foolery of gems:
Pearls like "Braes of Yarrow"
Let new Palgraves gather (and let
Me help my mother, if after

These aids she had no other).

3

I watched at last for her
Among our sacred
Stones, for I was grown
Before I found her tomb.
Today I point to that:
It's there my heavy mother
Rots. Remember!—
Of all the grades the last
Before the next is beautiful,
The lines of ribs, the grace
Of skulls, exquisite levers
Of her limbs; the next is spirit,
Musical with numbers of the flesh:

The formula of eyes'
Ellipse, the thrust
In the gentle eye's lash,
The figures of the listening
Fingers' nerves and of the
Foetal logarithm curves,
Of hidden colors of the guts,
Of buffered tensions of the blood
"Figured in the drift of stars,"
And pale Ameba's gestures.
Self forcing numbers
Enticed into her hyaline tips,
That stop in earth—and smell to Christ.

She suffers there the natural turns;
Her nests on nests of flesh
Are spelt to that irrational end,
The surd and faithful Change. And stays
To gain the faultless stuff reversed
From the numbers' trace at the Lasting Trump.
So here my mother lies. I do not
Resurrect again her restless
Ghost out of my grievous memory:
She waits the quiet hunt of saints.
Or the ignorance of citizens of hell.
And here is laid her orphan child with his
Imperfect poems and ardors, slim as sparklers.

February 1956
After a definition of Xenocrates and a poem of Richard Eberhart
and after lines of Eliot and Alejandro Carrion

A Century Piece
for Poor Heine
1800-1856

(TO PAUL CARROLL)

Give up these everlasting complaints about love; show
these poets how to use a whip.
—Marx

My forefathers were not the hunters. They were
the hunted.
—Heine

1

Heine's mother was a monster
Who had him trained
In business, war and law;
In the first she failed the best:
At work in his uncle's office
He turned a book of Ovid's
Into Yiddish. And Harry's memories
Don't even mention the family's
Chill and scare at the chance
Of a fortune from a millionaire. But a grown
Heine fainted and wept
If an uncle failed to provide;
And there was no money in the house when he died:

2

Except what he got from mother.
Syphilis brought
Its slow and fictional death—
Still he never would tell
His folks how sick he was of sex.

He wrote her frequently
To give no cause for alarm
Dictating because of a paralyzed
Arm, into the willing
And ready ear of some
Lady fair, reporting
For today, criticizing his wife
And telling the details of nearly-married life.

3

He called his mother a dear old
"Pussy cat";
His wife was a "wild cat";
She was the stupid Cath-
Olic opposite of the Jewish
Other—and cared even less
For his verse, being unable
To read and listening little.
Which is worse. Their need for love
So shocked him, he ran away
To a princess friend—like his sister
A rather crystalline dolly
Charitable toward sexual folly.

4

Two weeks after his mother
I mean his wife
And he were married, having harried
Each other for a number of years,
He put himself in a fight
With a man he got a cuckold;
He chose the absolute pistol,
But found he was only shot
In the thigh—and his own weapon
Of course went high.
So he went to visit his mom

After years of exile from home
Because of politics he put in a pome.

5
He left his mother I mean
His other at home
With her nervous bird and her
Shrieking tantrums—or else
He left the bird with the wife,
Et cetera—he wrote her a letter a
Day like a scolding parent
Afraid she'd become a Paris
Whore as he hoped she would
(And as he was) but she stayed
Till death, tho she shattered a glass
In her teeth, and all the rest—
Such as throwing a fish in the face of a guest.

6
As soon as he left himself
To the needs of a wife
He was shook to find in the face
In the mirror the eyes of his father
When his flesh had started to fade:
He began to be blind, and gave in
To a kind of paralysis that made him
Lift the lid of his eye
By hand to see his wife.
At the end, cones of opium,
Burned on his spine, helped him
To dream of a younger father
Doing his hair in a snow of powder;

7
He tried to kiss his father's
Hand but his pink

Finger was stiff as sticks
And suddenly all of him shifts—
A glorious tree of frost!
Unburdened of the sullied flesh.
His father died before him
Leaving him free to be
The Jew—he had fled their flight
To that of the protestant fake
Exacted in Christian states,
But pain had him lucid (or afraid)
Till the ancient covenant with God was made.

    8

But his tough old mother stayed on
And he never became
The husband; he took to his marriage
Couch interesting women,
Remaining a curious virgin.
In the last years of his life
He wept at the pain of lust
Stirred in his tree-like limbs
Already dry. And he left
Framing with paralyzed lips
One more note to his mother.
Only the ambiguous Dumas cried
At the holy rite they danced when he died.

    9

His soft old flesh slipped
Inside its great
Trunk with a sound he held
Too long inside his skull.
God absolve his mother,
His wife and him: after all
As Heine said, thrusting
Again that Freudian wit

He showed to prove to friends
And self his sanity had not
Come to the fate of potency—
"It is God's business to have mercy."

10
There is no need to forgive
His saintly poems
As there is for the work of another,
To whose New York park
The marble Lorelei fled—
Banned with the books of her maker—
To mock and lure at him
And us from a Catholic plot
Like a baptized, voluptuous mother
Powerful over the figure
Of the frantic Harry, and over the
Three mother-fishes:
Melancholy, an idol of the Hebrew Smart,

And one with the mended, broken arm of Art.

After Antonina Valentin
and after a memorial to Heine in Kilmer Park

Protest After a Dream

So what did old Diogenes find
When he took his lantern in his hand
And looked everywhere for a true man?

You tell me, for I
Am sick of tales
And books; I do not find
Your wide Dantean seas,
Your black, shimmering Alpine
Skies of De Rougemont;
I have not exchanged
For an Easter plain Raskolnikov's
Narrowing cell—Good God
If they cannot make us well, as it looks,
What the hell good are our books?

If Sophocles offered eggs
To a sacred snake
Or led the victor's dance
Naked after Salamis
He did more in this
Than in his poems, for poems
Are dreams and dreams are wants:
Our wants are what we are
And what we are is not
The man we hoped, it seems, so what
The hell good are our dreams?

Lines Against a Loved American Poet After Hearing an Irish One's Nickname

When Munson was in Paris Harold Crane
Sent him twenty bucks for one of Joyce's
Dirty books. What did *Ulysses* do for him
If he could only write while he was young,
Or felt he couldn't stand to face the boy
And woman in the aging man? Oh,
I know he lived an adolescent hell
Hurt by a candy merchant father
Who made his son wheel it in a cart—
A pimp who got a fortune from the itch
For sweets, which is like the itch for love
He didn't give. The dirty bum. The dirty
Father. What can you say? He was a dog.
He had his son's day. In the night the boy
Would stand beside his sleeping mother's bed.
Puzzled. Didn't know what the hell. Who does?
Who does. Still it takes particular heart
Not to eat the fondant of the sea,
That winking merchant attractive to any body.
Easy admirers have lied. A man
Cannot be a poet if he died.
They hold in them the feeling of the living.
I learn little, but he learns less from "Germs
Choice" crying in the wilderness.

New York Scene: May 1958

It is just getting dark as the rain stops.
He walks slow and looks, though he's late. It's all
Muted. It's like a stage. A tender light
In the street, a freshness. He wonders, a
Funeral?: at uncertain intervals,
Up the block, the corner, small, old women
Walk home with soft lamps, holding them with love
Like children before them in the May night.
A few people move down East 10th Street. They
Do not look at these ladies with their lights
Blowing in the rain-wet airs by the stores,
Their ancient hands guarding their ancient flames.
Three boys race out of the YMCA
At the corner, carrying the brief god-
like gear of the runner. Two jackets hunch
Over two kids. There is high, choked laughter.
The third wears a sweater, black as his head
Lit with the wet. They sprint across the street,
And are gone into a tiny candy shop
Half underneath the walk. A dialogue
As the jackets and sweater cross leaves him
One clean phrase, "tomorrow again." He grins.
He turns, pauses by a store with small tools
Held in half spool boxes in the window,
With beads, clocks, one hand-turned coffee grinder
And way in the back, a wooden Indian.
Now he stops a girl he feels he knows. He
Asks her where he's going, gives an address.
She teaches him, lifting her arm up, rais-
ing a breast inside her poplin raincoat.
He listens carelessly. He wants to see
The long, full hair that gives form to her scarf

Of a wine and golden colored woolen,
Like a child, some lengths of it falling at
Her back as she walks away, having smiled.

Concert Scene

(TO JOHN AND JANE GRUEN)

So he sits down. His host will play for him
And his hostess will come again, with wine.
He has a chance to see the room, to find
The source, defend himself against something
Beautiful, which hit him when he came in
And left him weak. On the baroque fireplace,
Whose stone has the turn of a living arm,
Some lacquer red poppies now are opened
In a copper bowl. Over the mantel
A warm oil against the white paneled wall.
An open coach; a girl and bearded man,
Both young, canter through a summer landscape
Soft with color, their faces full and flushed.
The Brahms on the piano is about
This. To the left a black coffee table
Topped with strips of crossed cane beside a green
Cloth couch. On this top a wicker horn leaks
Out white grapes by a tin of purple-wrapped
Candied nuts, and a thin white porcelain
Cream pitcher with a few, loosely figured
Very bright blue anemones and greens;
At the right of the fireplace a great teak
Desk has a red Chinese plume or feather
In a silver pitcher, then a clear, wine-
glass shaped, tall bowl—full of golden apples.
Still the music is Brahms: golds, blues, and wines
Of the stained glass panels in the far door,
A light behind. The hostess brings a tray
Of sherry and a jar of caviar
In ice, the thousand eggs writhing with light
Beside the lucent lemon slice. She sits

Upon the green or gold cloth couch. She holds
The thin stemmed glass, and now he looks at her,
Shook with the colors or the music or
The wine. Her hair is blue black and drops straight
From the part—directly in the middle
Of her skull—its long, moonwet waterfall.
Her smile is warm for him, lips large without
Paint, gentle eyes hollowed in the high bones
Of her white face. Now he sees above her
A graceful, black iron candelabra
On the white wall, green of its candles spin-
ning in the whorls of shiny surfaced leaves
At the top of a thin plant in the corner,
And in the jagged-necked, blown-glass bottle,
As big as a child, standing on the floor
By the piano. His hostess rises
To sing. (She doesn't know he's trembling.) Her
Voice is too strong. Suddenly the color
Is intense. And he finds no defense.

The Brothers:
Two Saltimbanques

Two boys stand at the end of the full train
Looking out the back, out the sides, turning
Toward each other. Their arms and shoulders brush
As the train shakes. They've been to the ballpark
Together, and can prove it with the huge
Red and blue scorecards in their hands. A sense
Of repeating in the shapes of the ears,
In the bearing of the clefted, young chins.
The older brother is perhaps fifteen,
The other, twelve? A gold of Indians
In summer faces, the color of their
Like hair, which is cut short, though with more bronze
In the younger. The brows of the older
Are surprisingly rich. And this young man
Is ripe with strength, his long face keen shaped,
Arrogant, rather sad about the eyes,
The face not yet tight. They wear green T-shirts
(Perhaps for some school sports?), their khaki pants
Sagging from the day in the sun. The two
Brothers slowly sway together with the
Motion of the train. The younger works hard
At his great scorecard. Now the older son
Bends to whisper: mixed, uncontrolled higher
And lower laughter runs over the train's
Screams, and raises heads out of newspapers.
Suddenly we strike a curve. The small one
Loses balance, and the other moves to
Steady him, leg and thigh muscles tight a-
gainst the steel weight of cars. They straighten. They
Smile, and the older boy's hand rests awhile
At his brother's side. Now as the train slows

A school of jets wings at the left windows
Tracking flame from the late sun. The boys lean
To the glass and the small one grins, gestur-
ing toward the planes, his long young arm poised,
Giving the lie to awkwardness at twelve
Catching for a passing moment the grace
Of what he felt. Now they move to the front
And get off. I watch them walk the platform
At the station. On the invitation
Of a vendor they buy Coke. They won't look
At the penciled dirty word, with its figure,
On the margin of a sign scorecard red.
They start home together for supper and bed.

The Picnic

It is the picnic with Ruth in the spring.
Ruth was third on my list of seven girls
But the first two were gone (Betty) or else
Had someone (Ellen has accepted Doug).
Indian Gully the last day of school;
Girls make the lunches for the boys too.
I wrote a note to Ruth in algebra class
Day before the test. She smiled, and nodded.
We left the cars and walked through the young corn
The shoots green as paint and the leaves like tongues
Trembling. Beyond the fence where we stood
Some wild strawberry flowered by an elm tree
And Jack-in-the-pulpit was olive ripe.
A blackbird fled as I crossed, and showed
A spot of gold or red under its quick wing.
I held the wire for Ruth and watched the whip
Of her long, striped skirt as she followed.
Three freckles blossomed on her thin, white back
Underneath the loop where the blouse buttoned.
We went for our lunch away from the rest,
Stretched in the new grass, our heads close
Over unknown things wrapped up in wax papers.
Ruth tried for the same, I forgot what it was,
And our hands were together. She laughed,
And a breeze caught the edge of her little
Collar and the edge of her brown, loose hair
That touched my cheek. I turned my face in-
to the gentle fall. I saw how sweet it smelled.
She didn't move her head or take her hand.
I felt a soft caving in my stomach
As at the top of the highest slide
When I had been a child, but was not afraid,

And did not know why my eyes moved with wet
As I brushed her cheek with my lips and brushed
Her lips with my own lips. She said to me
Jack, Jack, different than I had ever heard,
Because she wasn't calling me, I think,
Or telling me. She used my name to
Talk in another way I wanted to know.
She laughed again and then she took her hand;
I gave her what we both had touched—can't
Remember what it was, and we ate the lunch.
Afterward we walked in the small, cool creek
Our shoes off, her skirt hitched, and she smiling,
My pants rolled, and then we climbed up the high
Side of Indian Gully and looked
Where we had been, our hands together again.
It was then some bright thing came in my eyes,
Starting at the back of them and flowing
Suddenly through my head and down my arms
And stomach and my bare legs that seemed not
To stop in feet, not to feel the red earth
Of the Gully, as though we hung in a
Touch of birds. There was a word in my throat
With the feeling and I knew the first time
What it meant and I said, it's beautiful.
Yes, she said, and I felt the sound and word
In my hand join the sound and word in hers
As in one name said, or in one cupped hand.
We put back on our shoes and socks and we
Sat in the grass awhile, crosslegged, under
A blowing tree, not saying anything.
And Ruth played with shells she found in the creek,
As I watched. Her small wrist which was so sweet
To me turned by her breast and the shells dropped
Green, white, blue, easily into her lap,
Passing light through themselves. She gave the pale

Shells to me, and got up and touched her hips
With her light hands, and we walked down slowly
To play the school games with the others.

Shore Scene

There were bees about. From the start I thought
The day was apt to hurt. There is a high
Hill of sand behind the sea and the kids
Were dropping from the top of it like schools
Of fish over falls, cracking skulls on skulls.
I knew the holiday was hot. I saw
The August sun teeming in the bodies
Logged along the beach and felt the yearning
In the brightly covered parts turning each
To each. For lunch I bit the olive meat:
A yellow jacket stung me on the tongue.
I knelt to spoon and suck the healing sea . . .
A little girl was digging up canals
With her toes, her arm hanging in a cast
As white as the belly of a dead fish
Whose dead eye looked at her with me, as she
Opened her grotesque system to the sea . . .
I walked away; now quietly I heard
A child moaning from a low mound of sand,
Abandoned by his friend. The child was tricked,
Trapped upon his knees in a shallow pit.
(The older ones will say you can get out.)
I dug him up. His legs would not unbend.
I lifted him and held him in my arms
As he wept. Oh I was gnarled as a witch
Or warlock by his naked weight, was slowed
In the sand to a thief's gait. When his strength
Flowed, he ran, and I rested by the sea . . .
A girl was there. I saw her drop her hair,
Let it fall from the doffed cap to her breasts
Tanned and swollen over wine red woolen.
A boy, his body blackened by the sun,

Rose out of the sand stripping down his limbs
With graceful hands. He took his gear and walked
Toward the girl in the brown hair and wine
And then past me; he brushed her with the soft,
Brilliant monster he lugged into the sea . . .
By this tide I raised a small cairn of stone
Light and smooth and clean, and cast the shadow
Of a stick in a perfect line along
The sand. My own shadow followed then, until
I felt the cold swirling at the groin.

Nude Kneeling in Sand

The girl in the sand
colored hat
of unfinished straw
with its sides of waves
of water weaving
in the winds of her
yellow hair, her eyes
hives of bees, touch-
es her breasts toward her knees.

Like a child she digs
and buries
her thin hands in the
desirable flesh
colored sands, as small
animals or pairs
of birds that wait to
rise and stir scat-
tering streams of amber myrrh.

Out of ecstasy
her bright mouth
opens to the sun
as she lifts herself
to it and rests, with
breasts sweet and full, back
beautifully curved,
arms down, lap and
loins packed with moist, golden coin.

Lines to His Son
on Reaching Adolescence

I've always thought Polonius a dry
And senile fop, fool to those he didn't love
Though he had given life to them as father—
To his beautiful young boy and beautiful
Young daughter; and loathed Augustine's
Lecherous old man who noticed that his son
Naked at his bath, was growing up
And told his wife a dirty joke. But
I have given my own life to you my son
Remembering my fear, my joy and unbelief
(And my disgust) when I saw you monkey
Blue and blooded, shrouded with the light down
Of the new born, the cord of flesh
That held you to my wife cut free from her
And from my own remote body.
And I could fill you up with epithets
Like Ophelia's father, full of warnings,
For I have learned what we must avoid
And what must choose and how to be of use.
My father never taught me anything
I needed for myself. It's no excuse,
For what he might have said I think
I would refuse, and besides (is it despair
I reach?) I feel we learn too late to teach.
And like Augustine's dad I have watched you bathe
Have seen as my own hair begins to fall
The fair gold beard upon your genital
That soon will flow with seed
And swell with love and pain (I almost add
Again). I cannot say to you whether
In a voice steady or unsteady, ah Christ

Please wait your father isn't ready.
You cannot wait, as he could not.
But for both our sakes I ask you, wrestle
Manfully against the ancient curse of snakes,
The bitter mystery of love, and learn to bear
The burden of the tenderness
That is hid in us. Oh you cannot
Spare yourself the sadness of Hippolytus
Whom the thought of Phaedra
Turned from his beloved horse and bow,
My son, the arrow of my quiver,
The apple of my eye, but you can save your father
The awful agony of Laocoön
Who could not stop the ruin of his son.
And as I can I will help you with my love.
Last I warn you, as Polonius,
Yet not as him, from now on I will not plead
As I have always done, for sons
Against their fathers who have wronged them.
I plead instead for us
Against the sons we hoped we would not hurt.

A Trip to Four or Five Towns

(TO JAMES WRIGHT)

1

The gold-colored skin of my Lebanese friends.
Their deep, lightless eyes.
The serene, inner, careful
balance they share. The conjugal
smile of either for either.

2

This bellychilling, shoe soaking, factory-
dug-up-hill smothering Pittsburgh weather!
I wait for a cab in the smart mahogany
lobby of the seminary.
The marble *Pietà* is flanked around
with fake fern. She cherishes her dead son
stretched along her womb he triple crossed.
A small, slippered priest
pads up. Whom do you seek, my son?
Father, I've come in out of the rain.
I seek refuge from the elemental tears,
for my heavy, earthen body runs to grief
and I am apt to drown
in this small and underhanded rain
that drops its dross so delicately
on the hairs of the flowers, my father,
and follows down the veins of leaves
weeping quiet in the wood.

My yellow cab never came,
but I did not confess
beneath the painted Jesus Christ. I left

and never saved myself at all
that night in that late, winter rain.

    3
In Washington, was it spring?
I took the plane.
I heard, on either side,
the soft executives, manicured and
fat, fucking this and fucking that.
My heavy second breakfast
lay across my lap.
At port, in the great concourse,
I could not walk to city bus
or cab? or limousine?
I sweat with shock, with havoc
of the hundred kinds of time,
trembling like a man away from home.

At the National Stripshow
where the girls wriggle right
and slow, I find I want to see in
under the sequin stepin.
And in my later dream of the black girl's room
strong with ancient sweat and with her thick
aroma, I seem to play a melodrama
as her great, red dog barks twice
and I stab it with my pocket knife.

    4
In Richmond the azalea banks
burst in rose and purple gullies by the car,
muted in the soft, wet
April twilight. The old estates
were pruned and rolled fresh
with spring, with splendor, touch-
ing the graceful stride of the boy who brings the paper.

5

My friend has a red-headed mother
capable of love in any kind
of weather. I am not sure
what she passes to her daughters
but from her brown eye and from her breast
she passes wit and spunk to her big sons.
And she is small and pleased when they put
their arms around her, having caught her.
They cut the grass naked to the waist.
They cure the handsome skins of chipmunks and of snakes.
And when they wake in their attic room
they climb down the ladder, half
asleep, feeling the rungs' pressure
on their bare feet, shirt tails out,
brown eyes shut. They eat
what she cooks. One shot a gorgeous colored hawk
and posed with it, proud, arms and full wings
spread. And one, at the beach,
balanced on his hands, posed
stripped, in the void of sand,
limbs a rudder in the wind,
amid the lonely, blasted wood.
And two sons run swift roans in the high, summer grass.
Now I would guess
her daughters had at least this same
grace and beauty as their mother,
though I have only seen their picture.
I know she is happy with her three
strong sons about her, for they are not clumsy
(one, calmed, so calmly,
bends a good ear to his guitar)
and they are not dull:
one built a small electric shaft topped with a glowing ball.

6

In New York I got drunk, to tell the truth,
and almost got locked up when a beat
friend with me took a leak in a telephone booth.
(E. E. Cummings on the Paris lawn.
"Reprieve le pisseur Américain!")
At two o'clock he got knocked out
horning in with the girl in the room over him.
Her boy friend was still sober,
and too thin. I saw the blood of a poet
flow on the sidewalk. Oh, if I mock,
it is without heart. I thought
of the torn limbs of Orpheus
scattered in the grass on the hills of Thrace.
Do poets have to have such trouble with the female race?
I do not know. But if they bleed
I lose heart also.
When he reads, ah, when he reads, small but deep voiced,
he reads well: now weeps, now is cynical,
his large, horned eyes very black and tearful.

And when we visited a poet father
we rode to Jersey on a motor scooter.
My tie and tweeds looped in the winds.
I choked in the wake
of the Holland Pipe, and cops,
under glass like carps, eyed us.
That old father was so mellow and generous—
easy to pain,
white, open and at peace, and of good taste,
Like his Rutherford house.
And he read, very loud and regal,
sixteen new poems based on paintings by Breughel!

7

The last night out,
before I climbed on the formal
Capital Viscount and was shot home
high, pure and clear,
seemed like the right time
to disappear.

June 1959

Spring

of the Thief

[1 9 6 3]

Monologues of the Son of Saul

1

Ah so, our first load of honey heavy Christmas trees.
Then the sweet Christ comes again. See, in the high truck bed
the greens spring easy as the thighs of young lovers
while the aromatic golden gum, gift of The Magus,
oozes under the light cover of snow, rising slow
as the milk of the dead. Mothers will survive these rites
of birth, it is said. We prove it by our liturgy.
But I do not believe my own theory, and am cursed
to figure how I was blest at the root of my heart
by a man sitting underneath a flowering tree
in a white shirt open at the throat, dark face lucid,
saying the stories of a father for me. Yet I,
I have thieved my father's treasure. And I cannot pay.
On my naked birthday I brought to bed his amber haired,
shy eyed wife, her face birch white against the linen
loaf or coif of her pillow. Now, Advent, her quilted,
copper coffin glows again with a green, harlot's light
inside my head. Oh I've tried boyishly before to-
day to lay her virgin ghost in this enormous house,
but still I feel her black teeth click and push at the roots
of its dying blood (or apple) colored bush.

2

I did but taste a little of the honey with the
tip of my rod and my eyes were opened, and behold
I must die. May God do so and more my father said
for thou shalt surely die, Jonathan, but the Lord God
sent leaping from the heart of a bush a saving ram,
and so I live. Oh I have not my father's wisdom,
gift of a tender God to strike me blind in the road
and send me wandering, goodly monomaniac,
all one-eyed, over the oceans of Odysseus

(while my wife's fingers bleed as breasts on her unfinished web).
Yet though I have not my father's light I would know
my fault. For I did but taste a little of the honey
with the tip of my rod. Through God my life was knit
to his who killed the giant king with a stalk he ground
into the single, brazen eye: showering his blood
like rays of lucid wine watering the green slips of men.
I loved him as my own soul. I took off my clothes
and gave them to him, even my sword and bow and belt.
See, I have made myself naked for my brother. I
have made myself poor. Later when my jealous father
spoke to him alone at the table and had him play
the melancholy lute in his room, I loved him more
it seemed and took his part before the throne of Saul. Then
suddenly my father saw him enemy and sought
his life, the hot young breath of David, who won his wife
with foreskins of a thousand dead. When my father threw
the javelin at him, he fled. God what was his fault?
We sat at meat. I felt the cold growing in my groin
when my father cried for him, and so I lied for love
till my father called my mother whore and threw the spear
at me! It struck the wall. What was his fault then, or mine,
David's friend, who shot my arrow past the barren shelf
where he hid and turned the wrath of Saul against myself?
Out of a place toward the south my brother rose and
falling to the ground bowed himself thrice. He kissed my face.
We wept together for our human need, praying God
forever be between him and me, and among our springing seed,
for we but tasted honey in the summer wood.

3
"Far off the road on the left on a slight rolling hill"
I cannot eat my son in the tower of the barn
black with rain, though I lie on my back and starve to death
in a dirty shirt, sick and pierced in the flank by spears
of bronze straw, where he sits beside, his curious eyes

open in the dark, having twice dressed with rags my sweat-
tossed nakedness as I tore slobbering at my sack.
Christ I wish my sin in the barn had me drunk with wine!
Or that I lay in my chains looked at by gentle guards—
muscled, grizzled, Roman hero stripped and left to starve.
If a brown-eyed woman came to the barn in the long
rain, shivering with wet, child folded at her big breast,
I was too weak to talk. My son told I vomited
his stolen bread six days, even when he chewed and fed
the pap for me. (I know he cried as a child who tried
to keep alive some enormous feeble bird he had.)
No money to buy his milk, he said. I heard her breath,
felt her glance along my naked leg, and then away.
She sat hunched and silent, child across her lap. She rose
at last, and sighed: "Wait. I have to dry my clothes. I'll keep
the coat." And gave my son her child, moving into the
smoking, summer shadow of the barn. As she undressed
ah my God I could not taste again our ancient sweet
yearning in the flesh, now soft as underthighs of frogs,
and thought I was already dead. I wept. She walked close
wrapped in her wool coat of wine red. I shook my head. Yet
she lay beside me on the crushed, yellow shoots of hay
as though to rest, and loosened on one side her gold breast,
full as pears the drunken bees tremble for in the fall. She
drew down my giant skull. There, she said. There.
And I felt her fingers stir, weaving their life in my hair.

4
In my dream I know I see my father Saul a king,
the bronze gates of home shot open with a ram of oak,
my parents' private rooms naked to the look of the
enemy, cleats of their tough boots clacking in the halls,
packing the doors, where the mothers cling and seem to kiss
the wooden jambs in the hope of saints. The inner house
stirs with cries. The court shunts toward the cope of sky (and its
cold stars) the women's keening. Fifty bridal chambers,

extravagant boast for his children's children, their doors
thick with spoils of carved barbaric gold, smoke to ruin.
My father fastens round his aged, shivering breast
the dull arms of his youth, binds on his sword and sheath
and bends toward his death. See, beneath the open dark sky
a massive rock altar by a years-old laurel tree
that holds all of our loved household gods in its shadow.
My mother and sisters hover at the altar stones,
as doves driven by the hot storms, clutching husks of gods,
and when they see the king dressed in his rust streaked armor
Mother scolds him for his madness, asking where he goes
and sits him down softly by the sacred lights to pray.
Suddenly along the echoing colonnades my
screaming brother runs the gantlet of the enemy!
Chased by a mocking giant hacking at his young limbs
with swords. He circles through the court and long rooms and
      comes
last, moaning, before my parents' altar to pour his life
in pools as wasted semen or sacramental wine
shattered on the stone. My father cries that he has lived
to see his sons bled before his eyes like slaughtered pigs.
He curses my brother's murderer and flings his spear. It
rings the shield weakly, sticks and droops from the bronze belly.
The giant drags my father to the altar, shaking
and obscenely sliding in the blood of family—
he twists the old hair in his left hand, raises his red
sword in the right and buries it in my father's heart.
My father does not die a death of fame. His white head-
less trunk rolls on the shore without a name.

    5
If the half moon stamp of a sacred hoof showed Cadmus
where to found the town of Thebes, so what: Medea's love
has left me Corinth, as she careens into the sun,
her murdered kin (I think again of that hot, young niece
I had in bed) like a white and awkward albatross

about her neck—or like the dead ducks of poets, stretched
across a virgin lap. She fled mad in a flame red
chariot knit with copulating snakes, as the fake
staffs of medicine, rods of Mercury or Aaron
(whose brother came to life again out of a box a-
mid the holy human grass). It was this scene of snakes
god damned Tiresias to his female half of life!
So then my sweet son Bellerophon do not play mad
as David did, fellow in your art, who let his wife
lower him out of the house in a wicker cart. Oh,
I know how Saul himself (no artist) foamed in the mouth
and lay down nude all one day and night to prophesy
when David cut his shirt privily—he who played out
on the melancholy lute psalms of every man's heart.
The lame and ugly son of Jonathan, father dead,
and ignorant of his father's friend, sweat like a girl
to David's face, without faith the king had ever loved
in his youth, or first possessed the poet's gentle curse.
Oh my well loved son Bellerophon, you too have reined
the winged horse—your bastard brother Odysseus
lurked inside a wooden one, and waited to be born.
You would not stone as him the martyr Greek or wander
over his ancient, arrogant, labyrinthine route.
Odysseus I got on the daughter of a thief.
(The little, burnt moons I branded on the cattle's foot
printed down the road toward her house). Odysseus
was gored when he visited the crook, and you like him
are lame my son and beg for your poor bread, pushed at last
off the back of soaring Pegasus, who now is walked—
a tender-eared ass!—to pack the thunderbolts of Zeus.
You fell into a bramble bush like a horny saint
to blind your looking eyes and break the legs you dance on.
Yet no more than Orpheus or drowning Arion
could you escape the women, and one you had refused
lied like the wife of Potiphar—once you shot with lead
the disconsolate Chimera's female jaw, whose hot

breath smoked and began to melt the ore down her sucking
    maw.
Ah son, on the moaning beach Xanthian bitch on bitch
mad with juice they took from the smears of mares in rut, ran
at you, lifting up their skirts, to cut your manly parts!
For they hoped a poet's blood would fountain in their wombs
and make them quick. See, I weep for you my eunuch son,
beloved Bellerophon, and up the mound roll
back again the gradual rock of my grieving heart.

February 1960

To a Young Poet Who Fled

*Your cries make us afraid, but we love
your delicious music!*
—Kierkegaard

So you said you'd go home to work on your father's farm.
We've talked of how it is the poet alone can touch
with words, but I would touch you with my hand, my lost son,
to say good-bye again. You left some work, and have gone.
You don't know what you mean. Oh, not to me as a son,
for I have others. Perhaps too many. I cannot
answer all the letters. If I seem to brag, I add
I know how to shatter an image of the father
(twice have tried to end the yearning of an orphan son,
but opened up in him, and in me, another wound).
No—I say this: you don't know the reason of your gift.
It's not the suffering. Others have that. The gift of tears
is the hope of saints, Monica again and Austin.
I mean the gift of the structure of a poet's jaw,
which makes the mask that's cut out of the flesh of his face
a megaphone—as with the goat clad Greeks—to ampli-
fy the light gestures of his soul toward the high stone seats.
The magic of the mouth that can melt to tears the rock
of hearts. I mean the wand of tongues that charms the exile
of listeners into a bond of brothers, breaking
down the lines of lead that separate a man from a
man, and the husbands from their wives, in these old, burned
        glass
panels of our lives. The poet's jaw has its tongue ripped
as Philomel, its lips split (and kissed beside the grave),
the jawbone patched and cracked with fists and then with
        the salve
of his fellows. If they make him bellow, like a slave
cooked inside the ancient, brass bull, still that small machine

inside its throat makes music for an emperor's guest
out of his cries. Thus his curse: the poet cannot weep
but with a public and musical grief, and he laughs
with the joys of others. Yet, when the lean blessings come,
they are sweet, and great. My son, I could not make your choice.
Let me take your hand. I am too old or young to say with you,
"I'd rather be a farmer in the hut, understood
by swine, than be a poet misunderstood by men."

The Thirty-three Ring Circus

I /.

1

The wife of the clown,
a disconsolate performing goose,
is held by a rope
to a stake, like a hippopotamus.

2

The two and trio of hammer men,
torn dirty jeans and shirts,
poised black arms raised naked in the sun,
bow and gesture with the ancient grace
smashing iron stakes, in counter-
point of two or three strokes.

3

A carnival kid in white
cotton training pants
(perhaps the son of a gnome?)
is not spanked for fiddling with wires
at a socket on the shell of his home.

4

If we try to see in the curtains
of a performer's trailer, before
the circus, it is with the hope
of sneaking a look
at some slobbering freak.

5

An old, slop-hat, melancholy
father, no Telemachus found,
rushes weeping about the tent and ground.

6
The circus leopards start
electronic echoes.

7
The snake that can crush a pig
lies thick in a tank, its big
eye turning white, and its hide
which glowed with silver and red
on a sunshot Indian bank,
has begun to stink.

8
In the sawdust
nest of the ring
a small car spawns
a litter of clowns.

9
One grabs his hat and loses his pants
and grabs his pants and loses his hat
and grabs his hat and loses his self-
respect, his wife, and every mark
of his former art and life.

II /

10
The elephant, ill with fatigue,
straws of its bed on its back,
nudges in the ring
with a kind of stupid tenderness.

11
The camel, improbable
on the face of the earth,

behind the glazing eyes
in its small skull a dream
of sand, has placed its hump
thru a hole in a flag
advertising salad oil.

12
Not even shot
from a cannon,
the clown shivers
inside, peeks o-
ver the rim and
throws out
his human hat.

13
The woman in a blue bustle,
man in a blue blouse,
are skating on some thin ice
at the top of the house.
(Zeus crashing to earth
would take his spouse.)

14
The man stands up
behind the woman who stands up
behind the boy who stands up
behind the child who stands
on the bench beside its mother.

15
The girl has lost her face.
It blurs with her brown hair
as her body spins a sheath,
by the skin of its teeth.

16
The drummer, belly sweating
thru his shirt, conducts
with ease an inane waltz
of death or life on the trapeze.

17
Two fairies teeter
on the high wire.
In despair one leaps
over the other,
breaks his fall, and swings
solo, head over tail.

18
The man with a white parasol
walks a rope (in a white
suit) sloped from the floor
to the top of the highest pole
in the tent, and vanishes
in a cloud of light at the vent.

19
The lion hides his dung
and swings under his flank
his leather genital
unable to pump the furious seed
in a steaming African glade.

20
A harem of a hundred girls,
lavender veiled, their navels
and tops of breasts exposed,
beautifully die
before the stands, and rise
on ropes to Mohammedan heaven

where they play in unison
their tiny xylophones.

21

The man who
stands on one
finger, on
one edge of
a ladder
on one leg,
on a ball,
tentative
as a soul.

III /

22

Twirling her beads and plumes
she rears and jumps the horse
and tries to make him dance
(not a chance).

23

Unarmed a clown,
separated from the men
of his battalion,
is lost and shot down—
his dumb head blown clean
from his trunk. He trudges home
sorry and alone.

24

The giddy ostrich man
with his huge, orange ass
and bent bodice, his neck

hairy and slim (a gift
ribbon on its original apple),
scurries drunk and shy
avoiding our argus eye.

25
Clowns in adult, big feet,
red wigs and print dresses
with no hips
hang out their wash in the noon
August heat of the tent,
their sweating upper lips
hysterical with
hatred of their sons.

26
She swings out
into the audience
with swimming hair:
tights cuddling
graceful breasts,
her belly, and her
ravenous, universal
crotch—just
visible for an instant
above the crowd.

27
Black maned, the magnificent golden
Filipino, stripped to the waist, chest
oiled and smooth as a boy's, rides aloft
with his family. He takes the hand
of his wife, gliding past his brother,
who catches a perch and sweeps past him
to the wife, and they fly together
for a while till she exchanges them

in mid-air and he guides her again.
At last he turns toward his brother, and
throws a triple somersault, and fails, flop-
ping harmless into a nylon net.

28
Six ponies have burned
a circle into the ground
giving rides to kids.
(Their trainers trace
the radius.)

29
After the tent is down,
the circus owner, having
slept over, sets out
in his red car, feeding
his silver slug of a house
over the waste he is lord of.

30
Kids on bicycles
gathering bottles
and a dozen bent,
thirty-five-cent fans
from the Orient.

31
By a dead bon-
fire lies the charred
button-down
shoe of a clown.

32
Between the well
and the hill

is the skull
of a doll.

33
So gored a thousand times through the heart
and mouth and thighs our earth smells of the death
of worlds, for the sulphur dung of Royal Bengal
tigers, the droppings of birds of paradise
and thin llamas from the rare plateaus
mingle on the local lot
with popcorn and the vomit of a dog.

On Reading Camus
in Early March

*I discovered inside myself, even in the
very midst of winter, the hope of an invincible summer.*
—Camus

That boy in the red coat packing snow
mixes in my mind with the obscure
taste for beauty Camus's writing stirs.
I don't say the beauty of the boy—
open only through his naked face,
only his eyes drawing the full stores
of his emerging life, that seems to
root deeply back toward the dead. (See
how the boy stands footless in the snow,
like some smashed piece of Italian stone.)
Not that, but what he does to the cold,
pure seed or sand through his muffled hand:
how he brings the Midas touch of art—
I don't care how crude he seems to mold.
Not sad or old, not adult, the boy
has no more need of art than a saint;
and as he throws against the wall, shat-
tering what his hand could form, I feel
the older, more yearning child's alarm.

Song on the Dread
of a Chill Spring

I thought (and before it was too late)
my heart had begun to turn, that was
shut to love, for I was adamant
as saints, and tough as the martyr's heart,
as a wooden statue of a god,
where my father sat in the straight pew,
my mother bowed to the stone, bearing
flowers she had cut out of the earth
of my life. Ah the candles bloom cold
in the earthen air of early Mass,
like the tops of wan hepatica
that lift their light cups in the first time.
So shy we touch at these Ides of March!

Winter was too long and cold. The spring
is brief. These tulips offer up their gold
and the purple plum our grief.

Lament in Spring

Oh I have felt these same
yearnings in myself—
the tiny dark and yellow
hairs lit with wet
at the center of the May Day
violets Elizabeth held
in her seven-year-old fist
some six or seven years before
the grace she gave the afternoon

(her hand stemmed in mine)
at the topaz time of day
when children doze and she,
Elizabeth, waits breath-
less at the edge of the well.
She was my brother's girl,
and so I let her go.
For who can stand these old stirrings
in himself, and that one too?

Lines on His Birthday

I was born on a street named Joy
of which I remember nothing,
but since I was a boy
I've looked for its lost turning.
Still I seem to hear my mother's cry
echo in the street of joy.
She was sick as Ruth for home
when I was born. My birth
took away my father's wife
and left me half
my life. Christ will my remorse
be less when my father's dead?
Or more. As Lincoln's minister of war
kept the body of his infant boy
in a silver coffin on his desk,
so I keep
in a small heirloom box of teak
the picture of my living father.
Or perhaps it is an image of myself
dead in this box she held?
I know her milk like ivory blood
still runs in my thick veins
and leaves in me an almost
lickerish taste for ghosts:
my mother's wan face,
full brown hair, the mammoth breast
death cuts off at the bone—
to which she draws her bow
again, brazen Amazon,
and aiming deadly as a saint
shoots her barb
of guilt into my game heart.

January 23, 1961

82 /

Tale of a Later Leander

Great display guts. Fine young man come
from America swim Dardanelles which had
not seen daytime and especially this late
in year. I say "Yashaa" to this young man.
—Turkish captain quoted in *Life*

1

If thieves got your bags at Istanbul
you flew across the sea of Marmara
and banged on the gates of the little shops
at dusk, hollering for aid. The minaret
of a mosque, gathering the last light,
glowed above the blue-and-gold mosaic arch
like the torch of Hero at her point of watch
high over the killing Hellespont.

2

You raised the dead to fill your need.
You rode over the rock strewn plain for hours
near Leander's mythical home, to climb
aboard a scow manned by a mad team
of Turks, veterans of the cold swim.
The ship's cabin was lighted by a single,
urine yellow lantern, and an old Greek
steered by hand her length of thirty-six feet.

3

Midnight beneath an ancient Asian moon
you strip to the heroic, gold muscle and bone,
smear your belly and chest, swollen sex
and flanks with the scow's own engine grease,
and like a naked dancer poise—to dive
into the heart cold sea, its water
dark with Shelley's or Leander's blood,
its waves lit with pearls of their spent seed.

83 /

4

Your foot feels for the bottom of their grave,
rich with the silt of poet's earth,
Edward King and Hart Crane, and of other
wanderers to the sea: sailor, coral,
dolphin, anemone. And you rise again,
flesh flashing white! and black! in the pharos'
broken light. Eyes haunting, intent,
you start to crawl across the Hellespont.

5

Soon your bones cool to the core, and your face
aches and changes in that awful chill.
You rest on your back playing the girl
to the current and the moon, and drift downstream,
until you hear the Turks scream gibberish
from the scow, and turn to fight with the sea
again, heading north to the Bosporus—
moved as Io dogged by the lust of Zeus.

6

Once I hear you groan, see you are gone
beneath the surface of a wave, one hand
caught around the big, quivering stone
of your leg, stroking it, caressing
it, as a lost boy, toward your heart,
and treading water like a broken bird,
one winged. Ah, melancholy Icarus I feel
the sea's chill at the quick of my own skull.

7

Faintly they shout. You won't turn back
toward the ship, but drag your leg
as Jacob struggling with some abstract strength,
with Proteus, or the devil of the ice. Byron
circles his grotesque foot in the Hellespont—

as you watch the mouths of the madmen work
furious in the gaudy jets of light,
hearing how the cold has made you deaf!

8

A rope crawls on the skin of your back,
and you turn panic-struck into the phosphorous wake
of a black ship that bears its harrowing screw
just beyond, huge and spirit silent . . .
Weak as a tin boat you faint at last
on the rocks by the base of Hero's tower,
and the Turks haul up a frozen, shuddering, oily
beast of the sea: its twitching limbs still gesture
in the old, flesh-remembered motions of the swimmer.

On a Photograph by Aaron Siskind

Te Deum laudamus
  O Thou Hand of Fire!
—Hart Crane

1

After some miserable disaffection
of the only human heart and human hand
we'll ever have, we move to this pictured glove
or hand (ghost by absence) of Aaron Siskind,
a small spirit by image, able to shape

eloquently in the air—as though
to tell, "a man stands here"—able to meet
a handsome and beloved guest, or turn
so tenderly on a wife's face and breast.
Thus this glove, flecked with white paint that glints like

the unnatural light of an angel's scale
brushed off at Jacob's crippling, desperate fall . . .
pale froth on the wrist and palm of a proud youth . . .
or the pearls that whisper through the Doge's hand.
It is the left glove, the hand of The Magus,
of all who come late or by devious ways
oblique to honor Christ, all who have stopped
to see the sure, more customary king,
having set some ridiculous gift apart—
as frankincense or myrrh, gold for the child, art.

2

The glove's backed by grained wood
it is in some light held
molded at the lid
as the arm of a Saint in amber and glass
in another cast it rests

laid by with the love of a man
to be caught up again
or it will float out toward us from that rich wood
like the hand of him who draws life
deep into the massive limbs
of Adam gesturing
to name all the gorgeous animals of earth.
I know it is this hand
or glove of God that teases us
so that we must change our life.

3
Yet in certain lights it is a melancholy hand
sloughed off with the body's green flesh. It is the stone
glove of Keats, its thumb and first finger fast angled
in that last, inexorable geometry,
unable to tell a quill or fix the rush of wine
that has made the reader mad and left him graced again,
his face caught in a gentle, momentary peace.
Ah Christ where is that grave hand this glove has left behind?
Once it held a brush heavy with the hope of beauty.

4
It is a hand that has already waved good-bye.
By it we know
we have missed our joy.
The glove is waste,
relic of a little work long since done.
The fingers bend stiff upon the palm
for it lay doubled on them as it dried,
a dead hand of Nietzsche's dying god.
Ghost of the Master's hand!
Glove of Aaron Siskind! I
feel your canvas touch
flicked with lead spots of paint
upon the cold point of my heart.

This picture is a fist.
I feel it is a thing
Siskind had cut out of my quivering chest—
out of my huge, furred stomach.
It is a fist. It is a face
in the mirror I no longer watch;
and its light flecks have now the glint of tears
I have never wept
out of the tender, bald knuckles of my eyes.

Eight Poems on Portraits of the Foot

(After Aaron Siskind)

1

It is the wish
for some genuine change other than our death
that lets us feel (with the fingers of mind)
how much the foot desires to be a hand.

The foot is more secret, more obscene,
its beauty more difficultly won—
is thick with skin and
so is more ashamed than the hand.

One nestled in the arched back of the other
is like a lover
trying to learn to love.
A squid or a slug, hope still alive

inside its mute flesh
for the grace and speed of a fish.
Sperm in the womb quickens to a man.
The man yearns toward his poem.

2

With its over-long
profile lines of bone
and dark stem at the top
this African foot

is an avocado turning sweet,
or a hand-carved, upturned boat.

An idol carved of ebony wood.
I weave before it in the sand.

3
The broad, high palm ta-
pered, with its top
toes shadowed into a ridge

is like a hooded figure.
I find I don't want to picture
underneath that cloak

the hidden face of the foot.

4
One thick
foot is fixed
across another like an ancient

occult monument
of basalt
all of its meaning lost.

5
At the top of crossed foot branches
two rows or bunches
of small, fat birds are hunched.
Somehow they manage to touch

with tenderness. Short,
bundled up, squat
peasants,
they begin to dance.

6

One humped
foot, heel up,
lolls heavily on another.

Feet are members of a natural pair
and on these
(left and right)

sand has the glint of wheat.

7

The turned toes
in a rococo
scroll together form
continuing curves, one last line

after another,
with a final spiral of vapor
(or of light)
beyond that.

8

Held toward a water colored sky
full of birds and gods and souls
of the young,
the whole, lyrical foot bal-

ances, with its heel
on the great toe of its mate.
Watch! Next that earthen foot
will step into flight!

91 /

Spring of the Thief

But if I look the ice is gone from the lake
and the altered air
no longer fills with the small
terrible bodies of the snow.
Only once these late winter weeks
the dying flakes
fell instead as manna or as wedding rice
blooming in the light
about the bronze Christ
and the Thieves. There these three
still hang, more than man-
sized and heavier than life
on a hill over the lake
where I walk
this Third Sunday of Lent.
I come from Mass
melancholy at its ancient story
of the unclean ghost
a man thought he'd lost.
It came back into his well-swept house
and at the final state that man
was worse than he began.
Yet again today
there is the faintest edge of green
to trees about St. Joseph's Lake.
Ah God if our confessions show contempt
because we let them free us of our guilt
to sin again
forgive us still . . . before the leaves . . .
before the leaves have formed
you can glimpse the Christ and Thieves
on top of the hill. One of them was saved.
That day the snow had seemed to drop like grace

upon the four of us,
or like the peace of intercourse,
suddenly I wanted to confess—
or simply talk.
I paid a visit to the mammoth Sacred Heart
Church, and found it shut.
Who locked him out or in?
The name of God is changing in our time.
What is his winter name?
Where was his winter home?
Oh I've kept my love to myself before.
Even those ducks weave down the shore
together, drunk with hope
for the April water. One spring festival
near here I stripped and strolled
through a rain filled field.
Spread eagled on the soaking earth
I let the rain
move its audible little hands
gently on my skin . . . let the dark rain
raise up my love.
But why? I was alone
and no one saw how ardent I grew.
And when I rolled naked in the snow one night
as St. Francis with his Brother Ass
or a hard bodied Finn
I was alone. Underneath
the howling January moon
I knelt and dug my fist
full of the cold winter sand
and rubbed and
hid my manhood under it.
Washed up at some ancient or half-heroic shore
I was ashamed that I was naked there.
Before Nausicaä and the saints. Before myself.
But who took off my coat? Who put it on?

Who drove me home?
Blessed be sin if it teaches men shame.
Yet because of it we cannot talk
and I am separated from myself.
So what is all this reveling in snow and rain?
Or in the summer sun when the heavy gold
body weeps with joy or grief or love?
When we speak of God, is it God we speak of?
Perhaps his winter home
is in that field where I rolled or ran . . .
this hill where once the snow
fell serene as rain.
Oh I have walked around the lake
when I was not alone—
sometimes with my wife have seen these swans
dip down their necks
graceful as a girl, showering white and wet!
I've seen their heads delicately turn.
Have gone sailing with my quiet, older son.
And once on a morning walk
a student who had just come back
in fall found a perfect hickory shell
among the bronze and red
leaves and purple flowers of the time
and put its white bread into my hand.
Ekelöf said there is a freshness
nothing can destroy in us—
not even we ourselves.
Perhaps that
Freshness is the changed name of God.
Where all the monsters also hide
I bear him in the ocean of my blood
and in the pulp of my enormous head.
He lives beneath the unkempt potter's grass
of my belly and chest.
I feel his terrible, aged heart

moving under mine . . . can see the shadows
of the gorgeous light
that plays at the edges of his giant eye . . .
or tell the faint press and hum
of his eternal pool of sperm.
Like sandalwood! *Like sandalwood*
the righteous man
perfumes the axe that falls on him.
The cords of elm, of cedar oak and pine
will pile again in fall.
The ribs and pockets of the barns will swell.
Winds and fires in the field rage
and again burn out each
of the ancient roots.
Again at last the late November snow
will fill those fields, change this hill,
throw these figures in relief
and raining on them
will transform
the bronze Christ's brow and cheek,
the white face and thigh of the thief.

March–April 1962

Whistling Wings

or

White Turtle in the Watertree

1

"Whistling Wings." Jesus Christ.
Can you imagine that?
We thought we were so smart.
Had the turtle in a cage
for birds, till I couldn't stand the image
longer. Then we thought
the copper mesh around his pen would always flop
him back again
when he reached a certain point of compensation.
Like a youngster on a birch
he crawled up, catching each improbable turtle foot
(which the limbs of doves and wrens reflect).
But we must admit he won. He's gone.
Myth of the eternal return!
Perhaps he carries the world upon his flank again:
When we climbed up the back of Castle Rock
to take a long, leisurely look
all the maidenhair fern
shivered in the sun,
and the dry sweet pine
scales snapped like crusts of bread.
I felt the turtle's great wing shudder overhead.

Then again I saw the clams
try to put out wings
of a whitish meat (like small, phlegmatic souls)
from the Sisyphean shells

they always bear
even though abandoned in an auto tire.

The lean frog fled too.
Oh, we knew
he'd never feast upon the sun
blasted grass one kid put in,
wouldn't like the tone
of weeds against his precious slime.
Still we had a right to hope
he'd like the shallow hole
we dug, with its handmade pool.
But the frog's not anybody's fool.
Now (or thus)
as with Breughel's Icarus
I can see, in the green flowing
of my mind, his white, human legs flashing!
They leave a melancholy ring
like the abandoned whippoorwill's song.

He starts up at nine o'clock
each heartbreaking night.
The partridge has some sadness or other
knocking softly in his throat as a missing motor,
but the whippoorwill's music is the shadow, is the moon
of the last sheen of light in the meadow after rain.

The field itself leaves us blest
in an unrelieved length of pine forest—
like the baroque squiggle in the sand
of baby clams
toward water,
track of partridge with the cock's delicate trailing feather,
or turtle's print before (and after)
the shore has smoothed with weather.

2

Off the pine path
we found a pair of gray clad
wood cutters (work shirts and pants,
heavy hats
to keep off bugs and sun)
whose nagging saws had broken the peace of the afternoon.
The kids and I watched them
hack an arm
and leg from trees they'd felled.
"Pulp" I've heard the living trees called!
I held
my breath when one took off his hat
to mop the sweat
and suddenly instead a woman was there,
her hair
falling round a rather pretty face
gaunt with tiredness—
and in her blue, metallic eyes, as in a cage,
an absolute feminine rage.

There was masculine fury
at the Inn just off the highway
(like the inn of Joseph and Mary,
as the natives tell)
where a husband sent six Indians to hell.
The man and his wife, who had two daughters,
were the tavern owners.
He took the wagon into town for salt and bread,
came back to find his wife and daughters dead!
Four Indians had killed them with a tomahawk,
robbed the inn and were quickly drunk.
The husband slew the four
with an axe right there,
brought two more back

and placed six heads about the inn on pikes!
Now they have a marker at a wayside park.

3
With my own wife and kids
visiting the local Indian burial grounds
I find I wonder
at the penny-strewn boxes stretching over
graves recently dug
for Billy Walking Bird and Nora White Dog.
I would guess
a kind of halfway house?
They are buried on a low, wooded hill
where bluegrass seed and plum blossoms fall.

In another small area of cleared wood
across a net like that our turtle had
the kids hit a plastic badminton bird.

On a rope outside our concrete block cabin,
clean and damp and open
the many colored swimming suits sway,
all shapeless after joy.
At the beach, girl is clearly girl and boy, boy.
The motorboats buck across the lake
and root about the skirts of sails, who walk
by so slow
and turn so delicately now.

A blue and red and yellow and brown
and green and black paper chain
my daughter makes
to drape
across the drab stove in the corner,
each color repeating in a perfect order.
Yet this doesn't make plain to me

her genuine, womanly intensity.
See how she
bangs and shatters the dinner bell!
Which here is on a pole.
The house or cabin key now hangs upon a hook
over the kitchen sink.
These new juxtaposings make you think!
The baby's crib's back by our bed again,
and the other kids—blankets fluffed and clean,
shook from plexiglass bags—
all are rearranged.

4
At Whistling Wings our oldest son
gets up early to fish, for the first time,
or stands gold with summer sun
plumed in a gaudy summer shirt
like a splendid, tropical bird
none of us know,
to draw back his brand new bow
and shoot forever
the first slim arrow of my quiver.

That one late night,
only a hint
of moonlight,
Ruth and I
(our children all asleep)
ran down from the cabin to the beach
and dived together
naked in the summer water.
I asked her out to swim with me because
I knew how small and white she was.

His hair too long and yellow for the wood
the baby walks

quite drunk,
or else bending back
on heels like a pregnant lady
round and round a small tree,
or like a cub bear,
paws clumsy in the air,
nosing honey,
or like a grounded baby bumblebee.

Our young son Stephen looks
like a small anchor seated on the stoop,
his back to me, knees drawn up
and spread, arms hid
at some uncertain game he made.

     5
I have seen them strain and wheeze
to pull down young shoots of trees
they carry before them,
tiny drying limbs
held out,
as they circle slow and chant,
like elaborate candelabra in a rite.
(Once I thought
I saw my kids carried in their own trees,
parked there like ancient, shrieking harpies.)
And once in a low fog that rolled toward the wood
like those long sighs of the dead
I saw my charmed kids
conjure up or lose a voice, an arm, a head.

The girls put a puppet together
out of cork, sticks, string, and a feather.
They painted gentle or horrendous masks
full length on paper cleaning sacks.
And I have seen them push

or wish
a full cardboard carton
like a wagon
up a hill of sand,
and down at last
into the sweet valley of grass.
Have watched the boys build
a blunt sloop of board
and make it sail!
Saw one pound a nail
in a tin squash can
and tie fish line
to make a toy filled with stone
he dragged all around the cabin
yard.
Then (though I was gone) I've heard
our eleven-year-old
pulled an eighteen-pound
carp on a clothesline
straight down the main street in town
to weigh it in at the grocery store scale.
(Small, external Jonah. Revised whale.)
Once they nailed a brown bullhead
to a board
(through the snout)
and worked out his guts
having peeled off
the skin, like a man's sox
with pliers from my toolbox.
And they say the whole business is orthodox!

6
Except for the littlest one
all my sons
and I went out to fish one night.
Couldn't wait

to try a new lure,
sweet little thing from France we thought of her:
La Vivif.
No Jitterbug, no Cisco Kid or River Thief,
or black or flesh colored rubber worm
to bring the small-mouth bass home,
a weedless hook hid
inside its dull head.
Blue, red, bronze, and cream shapely *La Vivif*
would bring more beautiful strife.
We walked from the cabin east
toward the Ghost
for whom the boys had named the trail,
which leads to the water for a mile.
In the dead night walking near
we were startled by a startled deer!
Then, past a turn, at a sudden quirk,
that Ghost showed up in the germinating dark
hovering in the limbs of a ginkgo tree,
its great awkward silver body
like a snagged cloud
or enormous bird,
faintly glinting in the thin moon.
If it was a wounded weather balloon,
I felt it could still detect
the climate of my heart.
We joked too much (as they play
with bones on Corpus Christi Day).
Past the balloon, bird, cloud, or ghoul
we came to the walleye hole.

Putting that *Vivif* to the test
almost at the first cast
a good pike
flashed out of the lake!
I let each boy touch

the pole to feel the fish's tug,
and fought and landed it
luminous and foam wet,
the great eye without a lid
perhaps alive, perhaps dead.
Drunk with the success of our allure,
following some heady, ancient spoor
of ourselves or it
the older boys and I quick-
ly stripped and fell
into the cold, walleye hole,
like shining gold
bugs or clumsy newborn birds
hopping from a black limb (abandoned nest and shell)
into a blue black pool.
I hit a snag of weed,
was caught like an anxious white turtle hid
in the branches of the water's trees
for a long minute of time,
then dressed and went home.

Necedah, Wisconsin
Summers 1961–1962

The Zigzag Walk

[1 9 6 9]

The Zoo

1

Like a child the wise porpoise
at the Brookfield Zoo plays
in the continuous, universal game
of fish becoming man.

2

Llamas pray to the gods for snow. They chant
that it shall fall upon their artificial mount.
The llamas do not yearn
for tossed gumdrops or for popped corn.

Look,
even the great brown handsome official Kodiak
bear
has caramel in its hair.
Incomparable as he knows he is
the tough, tall golden lion looks at us
indifferent across
his molded hill, his helpful moat;
and, pregnant with a beast it ate,
the vicious, obvious and obscene
greedy-eyed old python
hauls itself along.

3

Gorillas lope and glare and crash
the glass in the Primate House.
The steaming place is packed
with folks who want to look
as at a wedding or a wake.
We advance. We retreat. We test. We wait.
We hope to see something masturbate.

We want to find a kind of King Kong
(magnificent but wrong)
caught and salted safe as us
behind the bars of flesh,
behind the glass of the face.

Twenty charming little tropical monkey kids
jabber in the phony trees. The gibbon is unkempt.
The yellow baboons bark, and they travel in groups.

There, ugly and alone,
awful and no longer young,
is that ornery thing
an orangutan.
Disconsolate, contrite,
red-haired widow who was once a wife
you pace and turn, and turn and pace
then sit on your repulsive ass
and with a hairy hand
and thumb delicately pinch an egg and
kiss its juice deep into your head.
Oh misery! Misery! You wretched bride.

Why only the silver monkey
glows and rests quietly,
nearly everything well,
a bit back in its tunnel
(which is lit
with its own created light).

This Primate House echoes
with our mixed cries;
it reeks with our ambiguous breath.
Each one caged as an oracle
I feel each upright animal
can tell

how much my life is a human life,
how much an animal death.

South Bend, April 1963

Three Moves

Three moves in six months and I remain
the same.
Two homes made two friends.
The third leaves me with myself again.
(We hardly speak.)
Here I am with tame ducks
and my neighbors' boats,
only this electric heat
against the April damp.
I have a friend named Frank—
the only one who ever dares to call
and ask me, "How's your soul?"
I hadn't thought about it for a while,
and was ashamed to say I didn't know.
I have no priest for now.
Who
will forgive me then. Will you?
Tame birds and my neighbors' boats.
The ducks honk about the floats . . .
They walk dead drunk onto the land and grounds,
iridescent blue and black and green and brown.
They live on swill
our aged houseboats spill.
But still they are beautiful.
Look! The duck with its unlikely beak
has stopped to pick
and pull
at the potted daffodil.
Then again they sway home
to dream
bright gardens of fish in the early night.
Oh these ducks are all right.
They will survive.

But I am sorry I do not often see them climb.
Poor sons-a-bitching ducks.
You're all fucked up.
What do you do that for?
Why don't you hover near the sun anymore?
Afraid you'll melt?
These foolish ducks lack a sense of guilt,
and so all their multi-thousand-mile range
is too short for the hope of change.

Seattle, April 1965

Two Preludes for La Push

1

Islands high as our inland hills
rise clean and sheer above the chill
April seas at La Push.
In a hush
of holy fog
the lean trees along their tops
(inaccessible to be climbed)
are offered up in flames of salt and wind.
And at La Push
the white, furious waves mass and rush
at each earthen island base.
These waves
are sudden, violent, unpredictable as grace.
They change White then
Blue then Green
swift as in Raphael's great wing!
I've seen it here where it has always hid:
Light, the shadow of our ancient God.

2

In the late afternoon light
even our human feet
start halos in the sand:
soft flashes of mind.
From the occult shore where you can see or feel
only a few shells
(shattered) among the lively stones,
we walk home.
I follow my younger brother,
for I am the visitor.
He knows the maze of fallen trees
that back up the blasted beach

for blocks: whether
this path or another.
Here the logs lie like lovers,
short by long, benign,
nudging gently in the tide.

Further up all the logs have died.
We walk through graves of wood
which are so oddly
borne out of the fecund sea,
each piece a last marker for itself,
each tomb planted with bulbs and whips of kelp.
Now as the water light fades,
I feel the monsters rage
again in this abandoned wood—gray
on darker gray.
Sometimes the flesh of the drifted face
is almost white! They seem to lift
their awful limbs,
broken from their lost hands.
Now the grotesque, giant shapes all
whirl awhile!
In the final light
the hard knots
of eyes scowl and brood
above the smaller dead
animals of wood.
I am afraid.
My brother walks ahead,
I reach for land:
the driftwood logs heavily shake
underfoot, and I awake,
balancing between my youth and my age.

Carmel: Point Lobos

"It's called God," he said.
He is young and he had
walked or flown ahead
to the violent crag.
"When I see beauty like this
I want to die for it."—
Jump
to the far rock home
where the white, roiling foam
seethes,
rolls one eddy on another, and retreats
to lie still
in a momentary peace or pool.
A little way above and to the left, the gull
folks form
quiet lines of their own.
They wait along the brilliant height,
and then, when it's time,
fling them-
selves off into the wide
arcs and dips of their angelic suicides.
Against the overcast skies
their wings and bodies
weave
a gentle, shifting spiral figure
as of light—like the faster
nebulae of froth along the blue black water.
Suddenly the sun is out; and colors
brighten all about the iridescent Point
with its prehistoric birds and plants,
Santa Lucia rocks, its hints
of whales. Everything's more intense!
I feel afraid in this

shattering new light.
Dread drifts like fog around my heart.
Why? The sheer, terrible height?
Eerie glint and glance of mica in the rock
which catches in the glittering sea below?
The rough, long time ravaged coast
here and yonder, yonder,
yonder
far as you look? Or the unlikely cormorant
never so near or rare, so gaunt?
I see the seaside daisy
die so beautifully
here. It loses its nunlike coif
as the lavender leaves fall off
and tiny yellow rockets burst
about its heart
till only the perfect-
spiraled flower skull is left.
Last I touch
(as if with hope) the odd, succulent lettuce-
of-the-bluff.
Its gray-white rubber flower
leaves a chalk stuff on my finger
like a soft kind of death.
I feel stark
as this Point Lobos rock
where I sit and wait, older,
while you climb higher
among the hundred-million-year-old boulders
in search of the precious nest. I rise
in this beautiful place,
look about me like an anxious kid
or a hopeful god
and give what I have into the sea ahead.

Big Sur: Partington Cove

the eyes of fire, the nostrils
of air, the mouth of water,
the bread of earth.
—William Blake

1

We three park by the Big Sur Road
at Partington Cove,
disregard the furious note
(ALL TRESPASSERS WILL BE SHOT)
and begin the long, dancing trek
—I mean a zigzag walk—
toward the creek,
the tunnel and the Smugglers' Cave,
hoping to return somewhat more than alive.
In the light air of early June
transistor sounds rise and weave thin
from the stream
where we guess the guard catches fish, or swims.
I'm glad one of us knows the signs
to find the old tunnel.
A large, white half shell
hangs from a branch with a hole
in its middle
(which has been filled with metal),
and a little farther on
hangs
a stranger
omen woven of many-colored yarn
and shaped like a little kite.
The Indians say it is "God's eye."
Now with our shoes off
we soft slosh
across the creek,

toes a school of fish.
A brief, final
push
through the young brush
puts us at the aged tunnel.
The guard is safely ditched, we hope.
Short trip
through the moist dark
under artful, handhewn
timbers, and suddenly we are borne
out onto the brilliant cove
the thieves (and landscape) made a secret of.

2

Hidden as the middle of night
still this cove is bright
as day. The drop is immediate,
sheer to the shimmering sea,
and now you cannot get down
to the little half-moon
beach
bleached white. Blackbearded thieves
and smugglers
swagger.
Dressed in the ancient leather
they heave and hustle boxes there
and pour
out of a giant demijohn
of green
glass flashing in the sun.
They drink and sing.
They strip and swim
and huddle round the small fire
on the shore
in their human skin.
Then they dive away and are lost

into the glis-
tening eels of water weeds,
brown and supple as a leather whip.
Oh these are men that could make you weep!
We see the great, rusting iron hooks
in stone, and the broken links
of chains they used once to shinny up the rocks.

3
The risk is great around the cliff
beneath the cave of the thief. I almost twist
to my own death
stretched in the sea's long and stony bed,
where anemones lie lovely as an egg
and open up their mouths like downy chicks;
where poisoned thorns
pierce the purple flesh of urchins.
We single file about the hill's edge
and the pointed, dangerous piles
of rock. At last we climb
to the high, secret, hollow eye
of the cave and drop inside
where the smugglers hid
and stayed
like tears we never shed.

4
Anxious here, shivering, I find I need to love.
I am the father in the cave,
and I am drunk as Lot was in the shelter
made of skin the day he loved his daughter.
My sons squat in the dark together.
I know they will not hurt each other.
My mind heavily reels in time as I hover
on my haunch like an enormous bird.
And now I rise and stir to find

what I can for lunch—
or for our life in this long dark.
The belly of the cave is large!

5

We eat and sleep
and get up to bathe
in light at the mouth of the cave,
while one goes off to think
alone on a point of rock
over the smashing sea. I watch
from my place on the slab of stone
in the sun
beside, where I lie like a lover,
father or mother,
and look over
his naked hills at the black, wandering seas,
or I shift to watch the face
of the sky with its crags
and beards of clouds.
I see the slopes of his weathered head,
and all the tawny
hair along his body
blows
and lifts like shoots
of fern or grass.
Gulls jabber about his nests.
Eyes hold the little lives of the sea
in their pools of blue or gray.
The starfishes of his hands loll and soak
the sun on the rock,
and his foot
juts out
like a foot-
shaped cactus plant.
(I want to touch or catch

the glowing thing that lives in the cleft
at the root of the throat.)
Muscles of the belly
break like fields along this golden country!
For like the lost or stolen flesh of God,
the self, more alive or more dead,
opens on to the truth
of earth
and sea and sky—
and the thieves' cave yawns empty
of our smuggled body.

San Francisco, May 1967

Homage to
Rainer Maria Rilke

(FOR GEORGE AND FINVOLA DRURY)

I love the poor, weak words
which starve in daily use—
the ordinary ones.
With the brush of my breath
I color them. They brighten then
and grow almost gay.
They have never known
melody before who trem-
bling step into my song.

.

I remember my early poems.
In the silence of vine-covered ruins
I used to chant them to the night.
I linked them happily together
and dedicated them
as a gift for a blonde girl,
a fine golden chain of my poems.
But as a matter of fact
I was alone,
and so I let them fall
and they rolled like beads of coral
spreading away in the night.

.

My mere desire shall reach
of itself into rhyme.
My ripe glance will softly burst
the stone coats of seeds

and my silence bring you ecstasy!
Wait! Someday the public
will drop to their knees
struck with my lances of light.
Like priests each will lift
the baroque chalice of his heart
out of his breast
and gladly give me blessing.

.

I am so young
I give myself to every sound.
My desire winds
its way
like the turnings of the garden
walk in the wind's beloved force.
I'll take up arms
at the call of any war.
From the coolness of this morning
at the shore
I will let the day lead
me next
toward the land-locked field.

.

At dusk, in the dark stone pines
I will let my shirt
fall like the lie it is
from my shoulders and back,
and pale and naked
plunge suddenly into the sun.
The surf is a feast
the waves have prepared for me.
Each one shakes like the last
about my young thighs.
How can I stand by myself?

I am afraid.
Still, the brightly joined billows weave
a wind for me
and I lift my hands into it.

.

O thou wakened wood amid the raw winter
you dare to show a brave sense of spring,
and drop your silver dross delicately
to show us how your yearning turns to green.
I don't know where I'm going,
but I will follow your needle paths
because the doors
I felt against your depths
before
are no longer there.

.

Put out my eyes! I will see you—
close up my ears! I hear you still,
without feet will go to you
and without a mouth will cry you.
Break off my arm!
I will take hold of you with my heart's hand:
Stop my heart! My brain
will beat—or ring my brain round with fire!
Still I carry you along my blood.

.

If it were quiet once—
if the casual and the probable
for once would cease their noise—
and the neighbors' laughter!
If the clamor of my senses
did not so much
disturb my long watch:

then in a thousandfold thought
I could think through to the very brink of you,
possess you for at least
the season of a smile,
and as one gives thanks
give you back again.

.

This is the day when I reign
and mourn. This is my night.
I pray to God that sometime
I may lift my crown from my head.
For my reward may I not once
see its blue turquoise,
its diamonds and rubies
shivering into the eyes?
But perhaps the flash
is long since gone from the gem,
or maybe Grief, my companion,
robbed me. Or perhaps, in the crown
that I received there was no stone.

.

Lord, it is time now,
for the summer has gone on
and gone on.
Lay your shadow along the sun-
dial, and in the field
let the great wind blow free.
Command the last fruit
be ripe:
let it bow down the vine—
with perhaps two sun-warm days
more to force the last
sweetness in the heavy wine.

He who has no home
will not built one now.
He who is alone
will stay long
alone, will wake up,
read, write long letters.

and walk in the streets,
walk by in the
streets when the leaves blow.

April 23, 1967

Three Poems on
Morris Graves' Paintings

I / *Bird on a Rock*

Poor, thick, white,
three-sided bird
on a rock
(with the big red beak)
you watch me sitting on the floor
like a worshiper
at your melancholy shrine.
All you can do is look. I mean
you lack any kind of wing or arm
with which to go home.
The three-toed foot of each odd limb
forms a kind of trapezium
about its edge
(though there is no web).
Oh bird, you are a beautiful kite
that does not go up.
You cannot even get down.
Because you've lost your mouth (it's gone)
only your great eyes still moan.
You are filled with the ancient grief,
fixed there lonely as a god or a thief.
Instead of limbs to bring you nearer
Morris Graves has given you
the sudden awful wings of a mirror!

II / *Spirit Bird*

Looking at Morris Graves' Spirit Bird
(1956), suddenly I
understood the structure of angels!
They're made of many-colored streams
of the most intense, most pulsing light,
which is itself simply the track
of the seed of God across the void.
Each length of light seems to be a thread
that forms this angelic or spirit
stuff. But it's not. It's finer than that.
What gives the light its substance and shapes
the streams into the spirit thing
(apparent limbs and parts of body)
is the heavy, almost solid and
somehow magnetic *eyes* of angels.
These create the dark into which they glow,
and pull and bend about these sweeps of light.

III / *Moor Swan*

I'm the ugly, early
Moor Swan of Morris Graves.
I'm ungainly. I've got
black splotches on my back.
My neck's too long.
When I am dead and gone
think only of the beauty of my name.
Moor Swan   Moor Swan   Moor Swan.

Lines on Locks

or

Jail and the Erie Canal

1

Against the low, New York State
mountain background, a smokestack
sticks up
and gives out
its snakelike wisp.
Thin, stripped win-
ter birches pick up the vertical lines.
Last night we five watched the white,
painted upright bars of steel
in an ancient, New York jail
called Herkimer
(named for a general who lost an arm).
Cops threw us against the car.
Their marks grow gaudy
over me.
They burgeon beneath my clothes.
I know
I give my wound
too much thought and time.
Gallows loomed outside
our sorry solitary cells.
"You are in the oldest of our New York jails,"
they said.
"And we've been in books. It's here they had
one of Dreiser's characters arraigned."
The last one of our company to be hanged
we found
had chopped her husband

up and
fed him to the hungry swine.
They nudged the wan-
ing warmth of his flesh.
Each gave him a rooting touch,
translating his dregs
into the hopes of pigs.
And now with their spirited wish
and with his round, astonished face,
her changed soul
still floats about over their small
farm
near this little New York town.

2

The door bangs shut
in the absolute dark.
Toilets flush with a great force,
and I can hear the old, gentle drunk,
my neighbor in the tank,
hawk
his phlegm and fart.
In the early day
we line up easily as a cliché
for our bread and bowls of gruel.
We listen, timeless, for the courthouse bell,
play rummy the whole day long
and "shoot the moon,"
go to bed and jack off to calm down,
and scowl harshly, unmanned,
at those who were once our friends.
The prison of our skins
now rises outside
and drops in vertical lines
before our very eyes.

3

Outdoors again, now we can walk
to the Erie Locks
("Highest Lift Locks in the World!").
The old iron bridge has a good bed—
cobbles made of wood.
Things pass through this town everywhere
for it was built in opposite tiers.
Two levels of roads
on either side
the Canal, then two terraces of tracks
and higher ranks of beds: roads where trucks
lumber awkwardly above the town—
like those heavy golden cherubim
that try to wing about
in the old, Baroque church.
The little town—with its Gothic
brick
bank, Victorian homes with gingerbread frieze
and its blasted factories
(collapsed, roofs roll-
ing back from walls
like the lids of eyes)—
has died
and given up
its substance like a hollow duct,
smokestack or a pen
through which the living stuff flows on.

4

So we walk the long, dead-end track
along the shallow, frozen lake
where the canal forms a fork
(this time of year the locks don't work).
And now and again we look back,
for the troopers haunt the five of us

out the ledges toward The Locks.
(We know they want to hose
our bellies and our backs.
Or—as they said—
"Play the Mambo" on our heads.)
We do not yet feel
quite free—
though the blue and yellow, newly
painted posts
for ships
bloom gaily
in the cold, and the bulbs
about their base bulge
for spring.
Soon the great, iron gates
will open out
and the first woman-shaped
ship,
mammoth, silent, will float toward
us like a god
come back
to make us feel only half afraid.
Until then,
though my friends will be gone
from this dry channel of snow and stone,
I'll stay here
among the monuments of sheer,
brown and gray rock
where you can read
the names of lovers, sailors and of kids
etched in chalk,
and in this winter air
still keep one hand over my aching ear.

Buffalo, March 1967

131 /

Thirteen Preludes
for Pioneer Square

1
At the aged
Pittsburgh café under the street
(it's open only during the day)
the ragged pioneers get more meat
for their money.
A coat and tie gets hardly any.

2
Cigarettes die in
salmon tin
trays of gold and silver
and you pour your sugar
from a mason jar glint-
ing in the morning sun.

3
Moe's loan
keeps the pioneers in wine.
There's a trail of blood in the alley behind.

4
In the Florence Family Theatre
through the triple feature
the oldsters sit and cough.
Or they sleep it off
stretched across three seats:
they laugh and speak
loudly
out of their dreamed-up movie.
Some wake and go to the john,
where they solicit the young.

5

In the Six Fourteen the queers
think *they* are the pioneers.
When they dance they bleed and swallow
trying to decide who should lead
and who follow.

6

Next door the highly dressed men
with their highly dressed women
go
into the Blue Banjo.

7

Indifferent or reckless
(male and female)
two pioneers hail
and meet.
Near the street
in a stairway
they make it, their way.

8

One aged fellow, smashed
at a corner of the Square
sits against the wall
(he doesn't stand)
and feeling the need
hauls it out and pees,
no longer a man.

9

The tall American totem
in this triangular square
scowls with its mask upon mask
at the Victorian shelter near.

10

The Square's mixed light
part-aged-gas, part-mercury unites
the drunk and beaten, swollen
Lady Indian
and beau a block from Brittania Bar,
the Negro weaving home from the B And R,
and the white man who can't
quite make it out
of the lounge at Rudy's Restaurant.

11

The great, garish,
painted concrete parking garage
fills in
across the street from the ancient building
where Bartleby worked and grew wary.
Its ruined lower halls have formed a marble quarry.
The upper floors are rich with pigeon shit,
and on a kitchen shelf still squats
the hunched up skeleton of a cat.

12

The oldest pioneer
still reigns not far from the Square
among tops, totem poles
on sale, little ash-tray toilet bowls,
lemon soap,
cups and knickknacks in the shop.
A real wooden Indian still stands
petrified at dying in the desert sand.
Six odd feet of bone
and tanned skin,
a purple cloth across his drained
loins (a little dry blood
is brown about the arrowhole above).

"Look Dad a real live dead
man," said a kid
and, tiptoe, tweaked
the king's mustache, which is red.

13

In the basement under the bars
about the Square
you can see bits of ancient stores
before the street was raised up in the air.
Pioneer Square
alone survived both water and fire.
Now the freeway named Aurora soars higher
and Seattle's ghosts settle in another layer.

135 /

White Pass Ski Patrol

His high-boned, young face is so brown
from the winter's sun,
the few brief lines in each green eye's
edge as of a leaf
that is not yet gone from the limb—
as of a nut which is gold or brown.

For he has become very strong
living on the slopes.
His belly and thighs are newly
lean from the thin skis.
Tough torso of the man, blue wooled.
Thin waist. White, tasseled cap of the child.

Beneath the fury of those great,
dark panes of glass, that
seem to take a man out of grace,
his gentle eyes wait.
(We feel their melancholy gaze
which is neither innocent nor wise.)

Like those knights of the winter snows—
with a healing pack
(sign of the cross on breast and back)—
serene, snow-lonely,
he patrols the beautiful peaks
and the pale wastes that slide like a beast.

Sometimes still blind from his patrol,
you'll see him pull down
from the dangerous Cascades his
heavy sledge of pain.

its odd, black-booted, canvas-laced
shape alive or dead, without a face.

Colors blooming in the sun, he
caroms down his own
path, speeds (bending knees), dances side
to side, balancing.
Under-skis glow golden in the
snow spume around his Christiana.

And as he lifts away from us,
skis dangle like the
outstretched limbs of a frog in spring.
He swings gently in
the air, vulnerable, so much
the "poor, bare, forked" human animal.

And now he slowly rises up
over trees and snow.
He begins to grow more thin, and then
vanishes in air!
as, high in the little boughs of pines,
the silver leaves flake silently down.

There are the shadow tracks he left
down the long, white hill
beside the lift. Wait! Look up! Cloud
trails in the bright sky!
Breathing a wake of snow ribbons,
something has just flown over the mountain!

Washington, February 19, 1966

Poem, Slow to Come,
on the Death of Cummings
(1894–1962)

*"I care more about strawberries
than about death."*

"Herr, es ist Zeit."

1

Lord, it is time now. The winter
has gone on and gone on.
Spring was brief.
Summer blasts the roots of trees and weeds
again, and you are dead
almost a year. I am sorry for my fear,
but you were father's age, and you were fond;
I saw it in your eyes when I put you on the plane.
Today it is too late to write
or visit as you asked.
I feel I let you die.
I chose the guilt over all the joy.
Now I know you cannot hear me say,
and so my elegy is for me.

2

I knew your serenity. Compassion.
Integrity. But I could not feel your death
until I visited your wife.
She is haggard with the burden of your loss.
I wish I had not come
before, when you were there,
and she served currant jam
on toast and you poured brandy in the tea

and laughed, slapping your thigh
and hopped, like a small, happy boy,
about your newly painted Village place.
Now the color on your walls and hers
is not fresh. It has peeled with the falling
of your flesh. Your paintings in the house already date,
especially the soft, romantic nude you did
(although I love it best):
Her dark hair full to hips,
girlish, unsucked breasts,
rather pensive belly, skin
a lucid gold or red like a faded blush.
Her beautiful, jet feminine bush.
And the limbs you made, thin with their own light,
with the glow of that other world:
Women. Estlin, your poems are full of love—
you wanted to know that other world
while you were still alive.
All poets do. All men. All gods.
Inside a woman we search for the lost wealth
of our self. Marcel says,
"Death is not a problem to be solved.
It is a mystery to be entered into."
Then you have what you wanted, Estlin,
for Death is a woman,
and there is no more need for a poem.
Your death fulfills and it is strong.
I wish I had not died when I was so young.

   3
Your last summer at your farm
like a young man again you cut down
an aging, great New England oak.
Oh you are big and you would not start to stoop
even on that absolute day.
I feel you are a giant, tender gnome.

139 /

Like a child you came home
tired, and you called your wife
asking to be clean. Still tall you tossed
the odd body of your sweaty clothes
to her down, down the ancient stairs,
and it was there as the ghost
tumbled, suddenly you were struck
brilliant to your knees! Your back
bent. You wrapped your lean,
linen arms close around your life
naked as before our birth,
and began to weave away from earth
uttering with a huge, awkward, torn cry
the terrible, final poetry.

July 1963–August 1964

On the Death of Keats

Lines for Those Who Drown Twice

I am recommended not even to read poetry,
much less to write it. I wish I had even a
little hope.

Send me just the words "good night," to put
under my pillow.
—Keats to Fanny Brawne

I do not care a straw for foreign flowers.
The simple flowers of our spring are what I
want to see again.
—Keats to James Rice

1

The last month in your little Roman house
your eyes grew huge and bright as those
a gentle animal opens to the night.
Although you could not write or read
you were calmed by the thought of books
beside your bed.
(Jeremy Taylor your favorite one.
Plato and the comic Don.)
"How long is this posthumous life of mine
to last," you said.
What is a poet without breath enough?
The doctor made you swallow cupfuls of your blood
when it came up
out of your rotten lungs again.
Your study of medicine
made you suffer more the movements
of your death. One tiny fish
and a piece of black bread
to control the blood

every day you died. You starved for food
and air. For poetry. For love.
(Yet you could not read her
letters for the pain.)
One night you saw a candle flame
beautifully pass across a thread from one
taper to start another.
All month you heard the sound of water
weeping in the Bernini fount.
You asked your friend to lift you up,
and died so quietly he thought you slept.
They buried you with Shelley
at a cold February dawning
beside his drowned heart
which had survived a life
and death of burning.

2

Ruth and I visited your grave
in Rome's furious August rain.
The little old Protestant plot
beyond the pyramid the Romans, home from Egypt, made
in the middle of the city.
All the names are English,
which nobody knows or nods to
in the awful noise and light. Nobody speaks.
This rain springs from ancient seas
that burst
behind the bones of my face
and wash in salt tides
over the small shells of my eyes.
Since my birth
I've waited for the terror of this place.
The gravekeeper in his hooded black
rubber cloak
wades ahead of us toward your tomb.

The streams that shape and change
along the tender's rubber back
light in the thunder flash
into grotesque slits of eyes.
They see my fright. Ruth's hand
is cold in my cold hand.
You, Keats, and Shelley and Ruth
and I all drown again
away from home
in this absurd rain of Rome,
as you once drowned in your own phlegm,
and I in my poem. I am afraid.
The gravekeeper waits.
He raises his black arm.
He gestures in the black rain. The sky
moans long.
His hooded eyes fire again!
Suddenly I can read the stone
which publishes your final line:
Its date is the birthday of my brother!
"Here lies one whose name was writ on water."
Oh Keats, the violet. The violet. The violet
was your favorite flower.

The Weeping

(FOR THOMAS MORGAN, 1873–1948)

Why do I still run
from the grandfather in my dream

I thought my love for him
died when I was young

Oh Grandfather you are alive
in the huge houses of my inner eye

Like the sudden yellow gleam
in the windows of your farm

When we come around the turn
and in the summer sun your high ancient home

Looms on the hill
I remember you cried like a young girl

Standing by the well
after Grandmother's funeral

Your mountainous beautiful
Welsh face all filled

And the roots of your hands still
Grandfather you blessed me once when I was ill

In my dream it was you who died
as I thought you did

And it was I who cried
as I never would.

November 12, 1963

Grandmother Dead
in the Aeroplane

(FOR ABIGAIL E. LOGAN 1875–1968)

Grandmother after that late eclipse
when I lay drunk in the weak, April grass
and watched the moon on the last, best Friday night
grow awful and cruel and then lean
slowly out of the light
(become an odd, dark rock
under which some of us
still have our moving lives)—
after that you can hold the very first
of your favorite Easters.
At least a good and gaudy card
came each year before you died.
There is no message yet this time.
Instead I feel you addressed
and mailed *me* on this Saturday plane.
Grandmother you have verified the myth
inside my head. . . . Inside my head
I carry your gentle, senile hunch-
back and your swollen ankles
still shuffle here in the airplane's halls.
Your rheumy, red old eyes leak out all our tears.
Look out, Grandmother!
Or else I will look in. The plane
window angles near us (well, between)
and your face
reflects. You are spread
thin and shiny over all this Holy Saturday.
Grandmother is there ever any Easter

without a hope? And will the moon
be light
for the Saturday dance again tonight?
I am angry since you've died.
The 727 motor at my ear
is joining me fast to Detroit
on my Easter trip,
and it has quite
disoriented my small, waning life.
Everything has died.
I'll learn how to mourn quite mad
if never to rave in love.
I want to stay up here forever,
Grandmother. For I am tired of the fogged earth
down there
with its esoteric itch of flesh.
"Time Flies." I swear my soul has just turned
ninety too. On the night I visited
and stayed
in your sad, old ladies' home
I really shook. Sick, I shivered
from the barbed, tiny animals of dread.
I kissed you and I cried
and tried to sleep
in the ancient woman's bed
(your absent friend) —
her family plastered to the wall.
Something flickered back
and forth in me, black and white,
and I touched myself heavily
again and again
to see if the young
man (I was twenty then) was anywhere around.
Oh you and I too have had our scenes,
since I was the chosen one.

When I was ten
and you visited the farm
you unwrapped your long,
red, lacy velvet doll
and then undid the bones
of china for its tiny house.
You took the picture albums
out of the attic trunk. And took that
milky, moon-shaped paperweight.
We squatted cross-legged on the attic planks
and swayed and wept for what
you made me think
the two of us had lost.
Was it really only you
who were not young
and who no longer had a home?
Oh, I did love you my ardent old Mom.
It was the second time for me,
my first mother gone.
You pushed me proudly in my pram,
and I remember this:
right in front of your friends
I wet my pants
until I knew you noticed me.
You fixed the rockers on my broken horse.
And just before the picnic once
put a poultice on my swelling thumb
to draw the sliver out.
Now I watch the nail's moon
blacken by my pen.
Look. My plane has never gone
far: it hovers in your air.
Christ what am I doing here?
Communing with you I guess.
Well then, come on,

my beloved crone. Open up.
Now I lay me down
in your aged lap and sleep
clean through this Easter.

Easter, 1968

The Rescue

(FOR ROGER APLON AND JAMES BRUNOT)

I doubt if you knew,
my two friends,
that day the tips
of the boats' white wings
trembled over the capped,
brilliant lake
and fireboats at the regatta
rocketed their giant streams
blue and white and green
in the sun just off the shore,
that I was dying there.

Young jets were play-
ing over the lake,
climbing and falling back
with a quick, metallic sheen
(weightless as I am
if I dream),
sound coming after the shine.
They rose and ran and
paused and almost touched
except for one
which seemed to hang back in the air
as if from fear.

I doubt if you know,
my two beloved friends—
you with the furious black beard
your classical head
bobbing bodiless above the waves
like some just appearing god

or you, brown, lean, your bright
face also of another kind
disembodied
when you walked upon your hands—

That as you reached for me
(both) and helped my graying bulk
up out of the lake
after I wandered out too far
and battered weak along the pier,
it was my self you hauled
back from my despair.

Suzanne

You make us want to stay alive, Suzanne,
the way you turn

your blonde head.
The way you curve your slim hand

toward your breast.
When you drew your legs

up, sitting by the fire,
and let your bronze hair

stream about your knees
I could see the grief

of the girl in your eyes.
It touched the high,

formal bones of your face.
Once I heard it in your lovely voice

when you sang—
the terrible time of being young.

Yet you bring us joy with your
self, Suzanne, wherever you are.

And once, although I wasn't here,
you left three roses on my stair.

One party night when you were high
you fled barefoot down the hall,

the fountain of your laughter
showering through the air.

"Chartreuse," you chanted
(the liqueur you always wanted),

"I have yellow chartreuse hair!"
Oh it was a great affair.

You were the most exciting person there.
Yesterday when I wasn't here

again,
you brought a blue, porcelain

egg to me—
colored beautifully

for the Russian Easter.
Since then, I have wanted to be your lover,

but I have only touched your shoulder
and let my fingers brush your hair,

because you left three roses on my stair.

Love Poem

Last night you would not come,
and you have been gone so long.
I yearn to find you in my aging, earthen arms
again (your alchemy can change my clay to skin).
I long to turn and watch again
from my half-hidden place
the lost, beautiful slopes and fallings of your face,
the black, rich leaf of each eyelash,
fresh, beach-brightened stones of your teeth.
I want to listen as you breathe yourself to sleep
(for by our human art we mime
the sleeper till we dream).
I want to smell the dark
herb gardens of your hair—touch the thin shock
that drifts over your high brow when
you rinse it clean,
for it is so fine.
I want to hear the light,
long wind of your sigh.
But again tonight I know you will not come.
I will never feel again
your gentle, sleeping calm
from which I took
so much strength, so much of my human heart.
Because the last time
I reached to you
as you sat upon the bed
and talked, you caught both my hands
in yours and crossed them gently on my breast.
I died mimicking the dead.

Lines for Michael
in the Picture

There is a sense in which darkness
has more of God than light has.
He dwells in the thick dark.
—F. W. Robertson

1

You are my shadow in the picture.
Once I thought you were my brother,
but to be honest, he and I were never friends.
(Even our boyhood secrets never brought us closer.)
Odd the way you stand behind and to the side,
like a shade. Still it is your own
darknesses you stay in.
You generate shadow like a light
or like an odor
falling from your arrogant shoulder,
eddying into your eyes.
The great eyes almost seem to glaze.
Look! They seem to tip!
Your eyes are alive with the gestures of death.
You've got something of mine shut in there, Michael.
I must enlarge the picture
and let it out
of your ancient, melancholy face.
My shadow yearns for peace.

2

You came to my house
just separated from your life,
your clothes still burning in the chimney
(fires tended by furious women),
books piled or bent ("She has made

me stupid," you said)
or lost. Dishes in boxes, smashed.
Pieces of your life gaped from paper sacks.
Shelves were stripped like flesh,
letters from your friends destroyed—
family scowling, all utterly annoyed.
Who was to blame?
Your marriage already gone
at twenty-one,
you said, "I have abandoned myself," and wept.

3
Something binds every kind of orphan.
I could find my own loneliness in your face,
hear it in your voice.
But there is something else,
some lost part of myself I seem to track
(did you know I used to be called Jack?),
so I follow like a blind animal
with hope (and with fear)
your brilliant, shadow spoor.

4
I followed in the sun
until we reached the silent pine
the day we climbed the mountain.
We were with your friends, Marie, Jim.
I was jealous of them
for they had known you longer.
It was then I began to wish
you were my brother. We cut
some sticks and walked behind.
Suddenly the pied fields, farms
and iridescent waters of The Sound
blue or black
simply fell away from where we watched

like the holdings of a haughty god,
and from the mountain top
I found an island in a lake
on the other island where we stood.
That is the way you seem,
there is your home.
Your eyes are like the inwardmost island
of that inwardmost lake,
and your tears are the springs of that.
Ah well, we all weep, Michael.
One of our eyes cannot even know the other
(except, perhaps, with a picture).

                5
Down the mountain again
we stopped to swim
in a cove of The Sound—the water
actual ebony beside the brilliant sky.
You walked away from the rest
for you had seen
another hill you hoped to scale
rising down into the sea.
Marie sat on the steps behind
as we undressed.
(She wouldn't swim with us.)
Tall, classical, you poised at your own place
on the stones black from the wet
of waves, and dove suddenly
into the heartcold sea.
And for a silent while
you were gone with no sign,
the time of a cold change.
Coming back you brought up
a part of the dark
of the seas in your eyes
and some of the blue, obscure snow of the hill

drifted on your thighs and arms
in the shattering sun.
Jim and I dunked briefly,
chattering and quickly pimpled.
We carefully kept our backs
to Marie as we dressed. You
simply stood, naked and plumed,
half hard
on the bridge of the rock
and (almost as an afterthought) turned
toward the steps.
Marie looked easily at your body
and smiled. You grinned
and climbed toward your clothes.
Suddenly I felt that she
had watched the dark
rich-haired shadow of me.

6

You and I, Marie and Jim
that night on the island shore
piled up log
on log on log (we couldn't stop)
and built a driftwood fire so big
I think it scared the four of us
into dancing barefoot on the sand.
The greatest fire we'd ever seen!
We didn't join our hands,
but the eyes of flames
grew huge
and struck us blue,
then red. Blue. Then yellow.
Blue. And as we danced and danced higher
the freshly made fire
threw our shadows each on each
and blurred us into a family

sometimes three, sometimes four
close as lovers on the beach!

    7
It was the last ember
of that transforming island fire
that seems to fade in your eyes in the picture.
It makes you brother, friend, son, father.
If it isn't death, it is change,
and in that fine shadow flame
what was locked is yours, Michael, as much as mine.

Seattle, May 1965

Letter to a Young Father
in Exile

When I last wrote
I was so hung up with old guilt
or fright
      I could not think
what *you* might need—you who are
caught by this fucking war
in another land,
gone from parent, from calming scene, friend,
who had to leave school just as that
began to help
          shape
the keen blessing of your insight,
which is bright and quick
with presence as a fresh, dawn-white
drop of milk.
      And now you have a son
whom you are also exiled from
double-walled away
          by
both an outer and the terrible inner fight
(more bloody than any human battle yet,
Rimbaud said).
Sweat, tears and sperm
press together from the muscles of a man
such as you are in our time—
an age which is only made
(it seems) for the old
who dare to send
          their gifted young
off to the predicted geld-
ing of a war, or jail, or to some other land

from which as you they never can
come back.
So you've become a lumberjack—
and undertake
the most dangerous of lumber jobs
choking, hooking, lassoing logs,
risking your young arms and legs
because you are not afraid.
Better to take the lives of bears and trees
than any of those
you feel inside yourself or in the eyes
of brothers, or in your own
yet unseen son's
                    burgeoning flesh.
He learns to nurse—
a sharp and tender boy
we have the hope to say—
and grows out guts, limbs:
desires to return what his mother gives.

Next, as do all kids, I guess,
he will try to learn to piss
with all the strength of giants, Gulliver
and Pantagruel, heroes who could stop a war
alone, or Leopold Bloom, higher
than two hundred fellow scholars
against the white wall
of his elementary school.
(Or the young man in Freud's dream
whose powerful river could rinse clean,
as in a famous, ancient marvel,
the filthy Augean stable.)
And one day your son will learn to swim and ski
with your own passing grace and beauty.
And perhaps in a heavy, red
woolen sweater and a massive, black beard

he will hunt swift and kill (as you) the lithe
heavy bear, and pose squatting alongside
its great, steaming, brownfelled thigh.
Michael, your son's rifle will resound
and resound
though you may only see his young kind
and not himself,
since you are banned, and since you do not have
his mother for your wife.
And you have lost one daughter or son
already, under
the murdering stress
of our own human hopelessness.
After the tender pulsing in
of your full tide of semen,
with the clouded image of a son
(which always brightens when we come)
once there
was the fusing of the sea and shore—
meeting of another half
                              life
to carry yours.
But then war
on the womb, solid hits—
and death for the quick new part
of you and her.
And now again the grotesque hidden scars
that form and grow in all our hidden wars.
With this slow grief and your present loss of roots,
with all your unwritten books
and your rock hard, exiled life
(its vicious, black, summer logging flies):
Jesus, how in hell do you survive!

And finally this, my own thoughtless role:
you write me a note

about your first son,
a bastard like the rare and brilliant one
of St. Augustine,
and in my brief reply I do not even
mention
          him. Well, I see (sadly) I am cruel.
And I too know how to kill!
For when I last wrote
and said I wanted to forget
                              (abort
your image out of my mind)
simply because you are not around
for my solace and my life, now
I see I raised what came
                    into my hand
against you. Thus
I am loving and as treacherous
as parent or as child—in the black
ancient figure you and he may fight to break.
Oh my lost, abandoned brother,
you know you had a father.
Now let your son
say so with the jets of milk
he has drawn from yours
and from the breasts of a mother,
whose fecund spurts
of white
as in the Tintoretto work
where young Hercules is nursed
by a god—have formed the brilliant wash
and brush
          of stars across the dark, inner wall
of our still radiant, woman world.

Buffalo, December 1968

The Search

But for whom do I look?
The whole long night you will see me walk
or maybe during the day
watch me pass by.
But I do not wander—
it is a search. For I stop here,
or here, wherever people gather.
Depot, restaurant, bar.
But whom do I seek?
You will see me coming back
perhaps at dawn. Sometimes
the faces seem like tombs.
I have tried to read the names
so long my eyes darken in their graves
of bone. (The bodies of our eyes
lie side by side
and do not touch.)
But for whom do I look? My search
is not for wife, daughter or for son
for time to time
it has taken me from them.
Or has wrenched me from my friend:
I will abruptly leave him,
and I do not go home.
For whom do I seek? Out of what fear?
It is not for queers,
for my search leads me from their bars.
It is not for whores,
since I reject their wares,
or another time may not.
Then for whom do I look?
When I was young I thought
I wanted (yearned for) older age.

Now I think I hunt with so much rage
that I will risk or lose
family or friends for the ghost of my youth.
Thus I do not know for what I look.
Father? Mother?
The father who will be the mother?
Sister who will be the brother?
Often I hunt in the families of others—
until hope scatters.
I will call up friend or student at night
or I will fly
to see them—will bask and heal in the warm
places of their homes.
And I must not be alone
no matter what needs be done,
for then my search is ended.
So now the panicked thumbs of my poem pick
through the grill. They poke
the lock
and put out a hand and then an arm.
The limbs of my poems
come within your reach.
Perhaps it is you whom I seek.

The

Anonymous Lover

[1 9 7 3]

Cape Elizabeth:
A Photograph

In pools
along the wide terraces of shards of shale
shot
    with white
amid the rock colors of a lasting fall
there
     are
       these very gentle moves
of life—
     a wonderful solemnity:
see the secret algae,
mussels and the mottled dark
barnacles
that open up their mouths like baby birds
among the darting, delicate fleas of God.
At the edges of the sea's expanse
loom giant clouds of silent ships,
and just on
       beyond
         the horizon
waits the little light-
ship I cannot quite
       see.
But watch with me—
for soon it will show up
in this filtered picture that I snap.

Only the Dreamer
Can Change the Dream

Riding on his bike
in the fall
or spring Fel-
lini-like twilight
or dawn, the boy
                    is moved in some way
he does not understand.
A huge gray or green, long porched house
(he's partly color-blind)
crowns a low hill: rise-
s silent as a ship does
before him.
The vision makes him yearn
inside himself. It makes him mourn.
So he cries
        as he rides
                about the town.
He knows there are other great homes
and other beautiful streets
nearby. But they are not his.
He turns back.
              He gets off his bike
and picks
        up three fragments of unfinished pine
adrift on the green
           (or gray) lawn
thinking—hoping—that perhaps
there is something some place he can fix.

Poem for My Son

1

Well, Paul, when you were nine
I wanted to write
and now you're nearly twelve.
For too long I have shelved
this fact
       in an
          in-
accessible part
         of myself.
And the presence of it there
is like a blush
         of shame or
guilt inside the flesh
of my face. A fall
bloom of bril-
          liant gold about
to wilt
     beneath
obscure,
      heavy breath.
Your breath is sure
as the hearty new born
filling up your bronze horn
in the junior high band,
and your cheeks puff with it.
Your pockets bulge with hands
as you grin in the picture
about to speak
balancing on the side edges of your
              feet.
I have seen your new

beau-
    tiful
body dive
and dance one and a half times
into the pool.
My mind moves back
to where at nine I sat
in the bus on the big girl's lap.
And more than once
                    forgot my lunch
so the one ahead
                in the fourth grade
(believe
        it
            or not
named Glee!)
would give me sections of her
or-
    ange
not knowing it was all prearranged
inside
        my mysterious head.

    2
When I was young
I lived on a farm Grandfather owned:
I remember in the cold
my small damp tongue
stuck on the hand-
                le of the pump.
My cousin Clark
and I got the calf to lick
us in the barn,
                but then
his father caught
                us and caught

172 /

us too smok-
ing big
      cigars behind the crib!
I carried cobs
         in buckets for the cook-
stove and cranked the separator hard.
Oh, I did
all my chores with a genial hatred.
Sometimes at night I lay
in waves
     of summer grass
feeling inside my chest
the *arching*
      of the search
         light *shin-*
ing from the distant town.

   3
When I was ten
        nobody said
what it was the dogs did
to each other, or the bull
(whom we never could
        go near) and
the cow with the gentle bell.
         The good
         nuns told
me (I didn't ask)
that my dick
could only carry waste.
But they were wrong.
My son, you shouldn't have
to wait
   as long
as some to learn to love
and find for yourself

a bright, a sweet, calming wife.
There are some things not all fathers know
but if I could I would tell you how.

4

Oh I remember times I wish
I could forget.
Once when the family took a trip
and stopped
                at a motel
you cried and cried.
We thought that you were ill.
Then at last you said
"Why did
                we have
                        to move
to this small house?"
And the vacation time
when you got left behind
in the car while the other kids and I climbed
the mountain side.
When we came back you did not feel
well.
        You fiddled with the wheel.
My mind's eye
                goes blank as yours that day.
And once after the divorce,
confused, you asked in a small voice
(a mild one)
Daddy, do you have any children?
I do, Paul. *You* are one.

Chicago Scene

(FOR ROGER APLON)

At the bar called
>   Plugged
Nickel in Chicago
red, blue and yellow hammers
on its honky tonk piano
easily make their hits.
A boyish drummer ticks
his brush
>   and pushes
back
>   a shock
>   of brown hair.
He draws lightly from his glass of beer.
A heavy scholar of the sax
mounts his giant bass
and together they begin
to snort,
>   smoke,
>   and carry on
like a Saint George with dragon.
This certain beat
pulses to the puff of Bobby Connally's cheek.
And now the sweet and sour sauce
of the old New Orleans Jazz
potent as our father's jizz
permeates the air,
seems to knock us in the ear
and starts
>   melancholy thoughts
(it is too loud to talk).

Behind the bar,
                    oracular,
a bushy bearded (black)
and muscled man
                    works
and broods. No one has ever seen
his face!
          For he's gone,
                              proud,
to the dark side
                    of the plugged moon.

Three Poems on
Aaron Siskind's Photographs

1

The louvered lids
of the still lived-in, hard
Roman House behind
(its old household heroes whole
a bit longer
                in the shelter
of their niche along the inner wall)
are heavily shut
                against
the sad, weathered stone
of the father and his shadow son,
whose curled head and torso have already gone.
The father's eyes still stare at God,
and his face is furious with hope.
His shattered arm once gestured
to protect
                his beloved son, now dead.
The father's still alive although the pocks
of time deepen and grow black
along his rock thighs, and time
too has broken down
his jaunty Roman prick.
But the stony hair remains
upon his belly and his son's—
like moss or winter wheat
as from the north of Rome
weaving from the graves of the brain.

2

Into the wet, brief,
                          green and white
flash of weeds
your ancient stone shade now leans
at dusk
sick as melancholy youth,
the blind too-smooth face
stained
with moss and memory both,
the strong, graceful feet first
taking on the color of the earth.
This ghost seems never to have had a nose.
Yet it has the bearing of a once
beautifully formed man:
Roman student, soldier, citizen,
toga carried back proudly
from the perfect, nude body
and hung loose from the young shoulder.
Now the flesh has gone slack from weather,
the face and loins made flat
by the terrible wedge
of a very slow sculptor,
and muscles of the back and legs
copied in an athletic prime
are made old and impotent by time.
A thousand and a thousand years since you are gone,
and then the long decay and death *of the stone.*
Must your face again go blank in a poem?

3
I could not decide
                          in this either hot or iced
weather
          or both (of the heart) whether
you stare wide-

eyed with fear,
               surprise,
                        or shock.
Sure it's a surprise
this leading so many lives
when you thought
                  you'd chosen
one of them,
            not
               two or more
or
   none of the above—i.e., tried
suicide.
         So I eyed
your nose
           again but could not recognize
whether it was aquiline
(as
    my brother, that tease,
used to say of mine)
or smooth, since,
                  as if by some contin-
uing token, your
                 stone
                       nose
is broken.
          The unfinished poem
moves to your mouth, sensual as a ripe,
thick-veined scarlet
                     fruit,
                          pert,
or finally
          just surly.
                      And is your
long, marble hair
                  a boy's or a girl's?

It is the two curled
                    lines—
one bright,
            greater,
and one smaller—
pouring out of your
                    mouth rather
                                than in
which seem
          to sum
                  or sym-
bolize
      what stone,
                  camera,
and poem try:
for these streams of water
gather
       back again
                  in
your teeming, unbroken basin.

New Poem

    1

The beautiful, bodiced

                yellow dress you had

and your long

           brown hair in the late

spring

     your eyes glint-

ing with wet

         that was not tears

(it

  was the moisture

of ferns,

      their

young, light haired fronds

unwind-

       ing, bending in the wind

together).   So it began.

We walked, we two, married (just)

in the Iowa City street

              quite aware

of our

     rings

        whose new gold, glancing

in the sun, seemed to make the fing-

er

  lighter:

      we hoped

they'd be seen by others.

We climbed on the bus and sat side

by side

     weaving

our hands together, reaching

for the feel of each

other
     through the small but fierce
intervening flesh.
Off the bus
       we walked on, and we wished.
Long, almost silent walk,
the always whoring or always virgin
sun
    blazing blue, gold, orange as it dropped:
and the long, inarticulated wish
like a many-toned print or watercolor wash
yearning, anxious, strange—
the eternally ancient
                (yet
in some sense young) hope for change.

   2
Just as the light
        began to be lost
we walked beside
        a freshly growing field,
and then at once turned
together as we heard
a very gentle, shuffling sound
with
    an unmistakable feeling of breath.
A breathing.
      Huge, dark figures were quiet-
ly moving
     through a gate
and spreading themselves still and
great through the field.
Some of them bent
      ghostly, beaut-
iful, to brush along the ground
with their long, lean heads.

Some few stood alone quite
                    self-possessed
in the failing light
                    and others stretched
themselves to touch.
                    The gate closed
as the last colt
                    lurched
slightly drunk or mad or wild
through the soft, half-light.
Then the groups simply stopped
moving
            and were caught
it seemed
            in a steaming
or fogged, fleshed and powerful tableau
in the twilight's
                    thickly purpled glow.
The meadow
            now
                    dark and filled
(I should
            say the fulfilled
field)
        blend-
                    ed itself with each of them
as we walked away
                    along the shadowy
disappearing fence

        3
to our first house,
                    Home.
The honeymoon room.
                    Structure now gone—
with my records, an

un-
gainly four-legged phonograph
                    with doors, height
and all that
          (a kind
                of absurd shrine)
and my books:
              a second floor
                        bay window
with a chair
          from which the libido
                        floats, looks;
heavy tapestried, linen
                    curtain
                        on
the wall behind
              a candled
                    altar,
for we were
          religious then.
And a bed.
          I took off my shoes
                        and wiggled my toes
lying on the floor in that first room
excited by them
              (toes I mean)
                        and fascinated,
flabbergasted
          by you—warmed
together by the presents of our friends
                    around us
                        in our new house.
Shy, we
      undressed separately
you in our room
              I in the bath down

the hall. "My god,"
                    I said
to myself (not quite pajama clad),
"This is exciting as hell."
The knowledge that my hard-on
                              would soon
have another use
                    than in the past
(terribly tired of loving a fist)
made
        me paradoxically calm. And glad.

        4
I must tell something more
                        of her.
For she gave up much to be with me:
school (she was a junior
when I met her),
brief affair with another lover. Family.
Her
    brown hair
                is long as I have said,
and that yellow dress she made
herself; besides she was very good
at seeing what is real and necessary—
a kind of
        anguished god-
                        dess at managing money.
She
    had the nearly haughty
look and bearing of aristocracy.
To tell the truth her
                    hauteur
half turned
            me on.
Invited to the Caribbean

by her father
              in the summer
she chose my own
                   less colorful, slowly drain-
ing ocean.
         The profile line
of her neck and face
had a Pollaiuolo portrait's grace.
And the aura of her presence and her talk
brought meaning, memory and hope
                              back.

     5
I was a virgin
            when
we went to bed.
             (Not that this
is
  so unique or sacred.
All of us were virgin once.
And many spend years along the fence.)
Oh, I know words cannot catch
much
       of the experience of sex.
On the other hand
painting, sculpture and music can—
the first two because we see or even
feel the textured flesh through them;
music because music's sound
like time
         moves behind, together with, or runs ahead
of spirit and mind.
It was the tenderness of meeting
that surprised me. Going
from my known man's land
into the flowering country of woman.

Part of myself moving inside you gent-
ly or thrusting, kicking like an unborn child
in its development.
Or like a live fish of silver or gold
now darting, now suspended quietly,
in your rich, profound, uncharted sea.
And you—you danced with me,
sometimes led
                sometimes followed.
I knew what loving meant
and for the first
time pointed myself toward your woman's heart—
tried to touch it with my groping, masculine hand
as I felt you grip
                me
                and ungrip me
with your closing and opening body.
You and I felt
                that we were lost
                                (or for a time spurned)
parts of each other now perfectly returned.
Predictably,
        I suppose,
                we
came too soon
                that honeymoon time
and shrank
        back
                into our own tight skins.

6
The great, bright, moon shaped crab creature
rests, having just crawled up on the shore.
Land leans away from the sea.
A giant cloud, changing shape, leaves the sky
black or blue or gray.

The crimson crowned, great eyed king is dead,
but long live his shriveled child!
Every troubled, dreaming young man
lets go the girl in his hand.
And the tired parents of each of us
turn over to sleep at last.

Poem for My Friend
Peter at Pihana

1

We all live
            on islands.
And you and I've
                    wand-
ered far this day
on one: on Maui
en route
            to Hawaii
which they call
                    the Big Isle.
I've gone farther than you have
because I find myself
catapulting away
from you as if afraid
                        to meet,
then back.
            Though it is
a horizontal zig
                    zag,
I thought
            of the vertical drop
of young men,
                a rope of hemp
around their feet
in the initiation ceremony
down a sheer hill
that (without skill)
could easily crack the skull.
We've seen the beautiful
                            pink

anthurium plant,
                    part of it
erect out of its broad
adamic leaf, the scarlet I'iwi
bird
        and the strange-boned
gorgeously formed
                    and mixed
native girls with hibiscus
in their dark hair.
                    That far
sheer, ancient wind-blown
                            mountain,
lush
        at its base,
                    its long
feminine
            erotic lines
partly shrouded
                    hushed
in mist,
        the sun sometimes just
catch-
        ing for a moment
the rocketing red
                    ohi'a-lehua flowers
which spring up
                    in the wake
of volcanic fires,
the yellow mamani
clustered like a family
                        of friends
on their stalks in bril-
                        liant patches
along hills
            and roads above

the native
>   houses
or the falling terraces
>   of taro fields that
run
>   stretching down
>   like quilts
or tawny animal pelts
toward the sea again.

2
You are patient with the pain
I keep
>   which I can
neither explain
>   (even to myself)
nor escape. And therefore I half
begin
>   to love you, as your
quick black hair
lifts as gentle
>   as your brown eyes still
seem
>   in the wind
that shifts from higher up the sacred ground.
At Pihana you stand
>   where Kamehemeha shed
the blood of young Hawaiian men
in thankful sac-
>   rifice
some few of his bat-
>   tles won. (He was
turned on to blood
>   by Captain Cook—
who was torn apart—
and he showed

191 /

                    a tenacity like
that of the later ministers
                              of Christ.)
The stones of the *heiau*
                         now
are the horrid black
                      of that
old
    dried blood.
Once before, you said,
                        you took
three
      of these
holy stones away
                  and they've
caused you more cursed grief
than
      you deserve, Peter, my friend,
well-meaning thief.
But there's just
                  too much
                            dangerous life
in these ghosts they've left behind.
Perhaps
         the sensual red Af-
rican torch ginger
should first have made you wonder.
For my part
I
  wonder if the urge to rape
an orphan child
                 and steal
his semen,
            leaving his bones all
broken up
           and black

inside the private temple of his flesh
is like that sacrifice
by which Kamehemeha thieved
young life
                for himself
and for the wife-
                        ly earth into which
it still soaks
                slowly back.
                                It
drips
in the enormous mother vein
or extended island cunt
left by lava tubes
                we found
and went
        through
                underground.
Kamehemeha had less *mana* than
                                his son,
you said,
        my guide,
                and less even
than his queen
whom he therefore needed
                        to approach naked
on his belly
        like a baby.
A thousand youths he threw
(or like a mad Circean swineherd drove)
over
    the Pali,
            Oahu cliff
of sheer
        fall and of
sure,

overwhelming beauty—
where the wind's so strong
it sometimes
                    hangs
you or wafts you back again
like a sorcerer's wand,
or like the spores of ferns
or the cork-
                    like
seeds of screw-pine
the waves will float
                         for months.
My own seas, my winds,
are weak today
                    and I
depend
          utterly on you,
who do not know,
                    so now
you walk
          suddenly out of my sight
if only for a minute
and I begin
               to trem-
ble with the panic of it.
My eyes drop at once
from this beautiful island place
to my own two feet
which I see
               monstrous
in their blackened socks
                         split
by plastic thongs
into two club shaped parts
like the frozen lava flows
from Haleakala.

The naked feet of Hawaiian
men
        and women
are graceful as their hands.
But my feet
are black and swollen
because I've died in this exotic heat
that gives
        life
to all other manner of men,
                        women and plants,
the hanging red
                heliconia, the hundred orchid kinds,
and tamarind.

    3
Peter, my absent
                friend,
the blood of boys, flowering,
may keep
        an aging king
alive, but not me.
I should have healed
                my grotesque feet
in the silver pool
in the valley of Iao
at the green root
of its great
        rising, aged pinnacle.
But I did not.
And now again, it's too late.
For Christ's sake
                Peter why don't you come back!
If you're really gone for good
would
    you at least

respect my wish?
On my Maui grave
I want someone to leave
a half-
        empty bottle of wine
(perhaps some food
                for our continuing need).
And don't let
        some kid
steal it from my tomb!
Just give me that
                blood-red funeral urn
at my foot. Perhaps an uwekahuna, wailing priest,
may wander by then
                toward home
and in the trained, spirited light
from his lean body
you will all see
the gorgeous white plumeria trees
that fill
        my cemetery up like girls.

        4
Thank
        God
            or Madam Pele
whose fiery
            goddess home has been on Maui
and is now in the still smoking
sometimes flowing
young Volcano where we head—
the desolation blasted stretch
on Hawaii.
            Or thank someone I say—
even Apua'a
            the lusty pig

god whose prick
              is like
a cork
      screw.
Thank one of them that you
are walking back in sight again.
I know you've been
                    looking for green leaves
to place on
            the stones
                    of the *heiau*
in hope of a safe passage
                    for all of us.
But please don't
              go
again, Peter.
              (That's my oracular
                          message.)
Don't leave,
            and don't let me drive,
but get me out
of this astonishingly bloody place
and after this
please keep such terrible beauty to yourself.

Note: *Haleakala is a dormant volcano on Maui.*
Heiau and mana *are Hawaiian for "sacred place"*
and "sacred power" respectively.

Dawn and a Woman

The morning
           island light begins
to grow
      and now
the cocks cry
           at giving birth
to the colors
           of our day.
Their feathers make the dawn
blue and red and green
and they will strongly brighten up their combs,
as in the cold lodges
our women drop
naked to their haunches
                     pok-
ing at the tepid fires.
Why, they will go out bare
to bring in another log
before coming back to bed!
The flames they build
as they squat
           and hug their chilling breasts
form halos in their pubic hair
                              for
they are hunched in the ancient shape
of hope.
      The fireplace
with
    its fine wisps
              of smoke
suddenly fills with peace
opening like
           the great, God-wide

                    canyons of Kauai
that drop clean from the clouds into the sea,
their distant threads of waterfall
like darts of light playing on the wall
and on the
                    body.
The woman will give us what she can.
We men will take what we are able.
(Painted blue
                    the Sibyl
inside ourselves is also writhing there—
some kind of dance about the same, uncertain fire—
I do not know what for.)
These early women, wives, lovers,
leave their dawning chores
and coming back needing to be held
                              will hold
us too.
        They already see
we do not know our fathers
and cannot learn to love our brothers.
But they will do what they can
                              once again
to warm our gut
                    and heart
and also that secret, incomparable cold
that grows upward from the groin
when we learn
                    we can lose a son.

Return to the Island

Along the back farm road the
Jacaranda
         and (still on Maui) the
Bougainvillea
burst like purple bushes struck with fire,
polyps burning under water.
                   And far below
the unutterably blue
"Sea
    of Peace"
bare-
    ly shows itself, a more
ancient symbol
even than the Paia Montokiji Buddhist
temple
       we just passed,
where a few
           chanting women sew.
Above us the
             fecund rain forest
and the weird loveliness
of the bright orange illness
on the gray Eucalyptus tree's
flak-
    ing bark,
whose fragrance fills
the twilight
with its bittersweet
           oils.
We walk together
        out of our
human love:
I don't mean walk *out* of

it, but
    within. Still we are more separate
than either of us might
wish at the depths of our lives,
and we leave our friends
                behind
in the car,
        their
lives and limbs entwined
like the roots of trees
apparently
            beautiful as the name of
that one: Macadamia.
Or Avocado.
And the slow,
gray sheep whose coats begin to glow
in the going light,
their faces start-
                ling black
as they make
their yearning, childlike
                music;
and the yet
            blacker cows with faces white
as mimes
            amble up
                to us
pleased with the grass
                we pull
from beside the road
and toss
into their field; in their shud-
                        dering ancient peace
these cows and sheep
quietly take their fill.
I feel

It is our love that must
                    just
nibble at the exotic hill.
There is a white
upper
        half-flower
where we walk
(whose bloom is now growing dark),
the Naupaka of the Hill.
The Naupaka of the Sea turns its other half-circle
of lower petals
from the dis-
                tant Pacific
this
    way.
Is it because of me
we both seem Naupakas of the Hill?
Or is it because of imperfect
                        human love it-
self
    we
seem two Naupakas of the Sea?

Poem:

Tears, Spray, and Steam

(IN MEMORIAM: ERIC BARKER)

1

Peering, stung,
              bleared, hung-
over and lame,
through the waves of spray,
I feel somewhat
              panicky,
weird, about my sweat-
              ing body.
For where do we and our vapors end?
Where does the bath begin?

Strange to be able to see through the steam
(but satisfying to the point of calm,
like the vision of the perfect, new born)
for the first time
the whole,
              beautiful body of a friend.

Like a god
              damned eternal thief
of heat,
       clouds
wreathing round
your black, bearded head,
belly, limbs and your sex
(but no piercing eagle about,
yet)
you lie flat on your back

on the rock
            ledge bench in the bath,
Promethean in your black
                        wrath.

    2
In our nun's or monk's
                black
rubber hoods
(lace-paper coifs
                just visible at the tops
of our heads),
as if about to pray,
and black rubber coats
                to our feet
because of the spray,
we walk the Niagara Tunnel.
You can tell
            almost for sure
which ones the kids are,
but you can't tell men from women here.
Unsexed in these catacombs we watch
for the asperges of the bath.
The damp walls bleed rice.
All dark, all si-
                lent, we all pass.
We bow, each to each,
and some,
        not only young,
give the ancient kiss of peace,
standing in the alcoves again.
We reach for rain.
The Falls' spray touches each of us.
The glass
            over our eyes
                    weeps.

Cheeks
       are wet. Lips.
Even our teeth if our mouths gape.
We are caress-
            ed with wetness
all about our cloaks,
and we sway
          and float
broken out in a dark sweat,
complex, prodigious:
female, white, male, black, lay, religious.
At last we all
           peer out the stone holes
at the back of the Falls
and see nothing but The Existential Wall:
water roaring out of the hidden hills.
Power passes us, detached,
              abstract,
except for this cold steam
that licks and teases
           until at last
we turn our drenched, glistening backs.

   3
Aging, still
       agile
poet Eric Barker,
who has been coming
(I almost said springing)
back here
       for many years,
and I and two friends
strip at the still springs
with their
       full smell of sulphur—
here where bodies and warm water

are moon- and candle-lit, wind woven,
in a shallow cavern
                    open
to the heaving, iridescent sea
near
     Big Sur,
and we invade the great,
                         Roman bath
intimidat-
ing the Esalen teacher with his small class:
three naked girls in three corners of the big tub—
he, their leader,
               in the other.
The candles waver
as the class takes cover
                      and the mad teacher
leaves with one student to find
a night watchman, leaving behind
the others:
           one of them
already slithers
in a smaller tub with one of our friends.
The third girl now fully dressed—
and for the moment repress-
ed—stares
          at the rest of us
lolling and floating our masculine flowers
as we give a naked reading of William Butler
Yeats to each other
                   (taking care not
to get the book wet)
and then we read to her
as she begins to listen.
                       So she too strips and
slips into the fourth corner,
becomes for a moment our teacher.

Her breasts come alive in the water.
Yeats
     will wait
and Keats—for Barker, with whom
we have been drinking wine
all afternoon
knows
     all the Odes
         by heart
as well as many
         bawdy songs:
"My long
     delayed erection,"
he'd recited, laughing,
"rises in the wrong direction."
But he too is silent
for the while, and
         sits stately,
buoyed by the
         water: its movement
makes his white
body hair seem to sprout.
Soon,
     we begin
         to say the poems again
and to touch each other—
         the older
man, me,
the boys and the girls read-
ing over the sea's
sounds
     by the candles'
light and the moon bright, burgeoning,
shin-
     ing time to time
         as

the clouds pass.
                    In this gently flash-
ing light then
we all leave the tubs and run
dripping down the shore
together before
            any others come—
as hostile teacher, watchman.
But in that warm spring
water which we briefly left, everything
                            eventually heals:
for, by
        the sea
it flows out of these ancient, California hills,
which are the trans-
                        formed,
giant body of a once
powerful, feather, bone and turquoise-adorned
Indian Prince,
                and the sulphur is the changed
sharp incense
                he burned daily as he chanted
year and year over for the sick young princess—
who took her loveliness
from the many-colored, fragrant trees
and the flickering sea.
Finally, unable to help,
                    he thought,
the tawny-skinned prince
died of his grief,
and his body became this mount-
ain. And everybody here who comes together
                                in belief
is somehow bound, bathed,
                    and made

whole, e-
        ven as was she
by this gradual, glinting water,
the prince's continual tears for his sister.

So, when we return a little later
from our dance along the open shore
we find the Esalen
        teacher there again,
and the watchman,
each with a woman.
They wait
        in that gentle, lunatic light for us.
They smile as they undress.
Eric Barker takes a leak,
begins reciting Keats,
and we all bathe and sing together
in the new waters of brother, sister.

S0-ABD-063

A PLACE
like this

steven herrick

Simon Pulse
New York London Toronto Sydney

**Dedicated to Leonie Tyle, Robyn Sheahan,
and Glen Leitch for their support and belief.**

If you purchased this book without a cover, you should be aware
that this book is stolen property. It was reported "unsold and
destroyed" to the publisher, and neither the author nor the
publisher has received any payment for this "stripped book."

This book is a work of fiction. Any references to historical
events, real people, or real locales are used fictitiously. Other
names, characters, places, and incidents are the product of the
author's imagination, and any resemblance to actual events or
locales or persons, living or dead, is entirely coincidental.

First Simon Pulse edition March 2004

Copyright © 1998 by Steven Herrick
Published by arrangement with University of Queensland Press
Originally published in Australia in 1998 by University of
Queensland Press

SIMON PULSE
An imprint of Simon & Schuster
Children's Publishing Division
1230 Avenue of the Americas
New York, NY 10020

All rights reserved, including the right of
reproduction in whole or in part in any form.

Printed in the United States of America

10 9 8 7 6 5 4 3 2 1

Library of Congress Control Number 2003110836

ISBN 0-689-87112-0 (Simon Pulse pbk.)

CONTENTS

a place like this

weird

a young orchard

Go

*J*ack

I'm not unemployed.
I'm just not working at the moment.
School now seems a distant shame
    of ball games, half-lies at lunch time,
    and teachers fearing the worst.
I'm not studying either.
Yeah, I got into Uni,
    so did Annabel.
Two Arts degrees does not a life make.
So we both chucked it.
University is too serious.
I'm eighteen years old,
    too young to work forever
    too old to stay home.
Annabel and I make love most afternoons,
    which, as you can imagine,
    passes the time
    but
I don't think we can make money out of it,
or learn much, although, we have learnt something ...

I want to leave town
I want to leave town
I want to leave.

*J*ack's Dad

What can I tell you about my Dad?
Years ago I would have said
an ill-fitting suit, brown shoes,
a haircut of nightmares,
and a job, in the city.
That's all.
That's what I would have said.
And a dead wife.
Long dead. Dead yesterday.
No difference.

But not now.
Now, he tries.
He reads the paper with courage.
He never shakes his head when I'm late home.
He's forty-two years of hope
    eight years of grief, and
    two years of struggle.

Let me tell you this one thing about my father,
and leave it at that.

Friday night, two months ago.
I'm trying to sleep,
when I hear this soft bounce, every few seconds,
and the backyard floodlight is on.

It's midnight,
and there's a man in the yard.
I grab the cricket bat from the hall cupboard,
check my sister's room, she's asleep,
still in her Levi's and black top
(I like that top — I gave it to her
for her birthday, and she always wears it.
Sorry, I better go bash this burglar ...)

Where's my father when the house needs defending?
At the pub? At work?
Not at midnight surely?
I grip the bat,
wish I'd taken cricket more seriously at school.
I open the door slightly,
think of newspaper headlines —
"HERO DIES SAVING HOUSE"
"CRIME WAVE SOARS OUT WEST"
"HIT FOR SIX!"

There's that bounce again,
and the figure bends to pick something up
(a gun! a knife!)

A cricket ball!
What!

4

He runs and bowls a
slow drifting leg-spinner, hits middle stump.
Dad turns,
whispers "howzat!"
and walks to pick up the ball again.

What can I do?
My Dad, midnight cricket,
and a well-flighted leg-spinner.

I walk out to face up
tapping the bat gently.
Dad smiles and bowls a wrong-un.
The bastard knocks my off-stump out.
He offers me a handshake and advice.
"Bat and pad together son,
   don't leave the gate open.
   Let's have one more over shall we?"

He goes back to his mark,
polishing the ball on his pyjamas,
every nerve twitching,
every breath involved.

The stumbling bagpipes

We make love every Tuesday afternoon.
I kiss her eyelids
and rub my hand along her arm
to feel the soft hair
that shines in the fading light.
Sometimes the clouds float
up the valley
and the rain dances on our window
as the parrots fly for home.
I kiss her shoulders and her neck
and we try breathing slowly, in time,
under the doona.

There's a young boy next door
who's practicing the bagpipes.
He stands on the veranda
and scares hell out of the dogs.
They howl in time
as he blows himself hoarse.

We love that sound,
discordant, clumsy, feverish.
It reminds us of that first Tuesday afternoon,
two years ago,

trying to make love before
Annabel's parents got home.
We agreed on further practice.

That's why we celebrate like this,
every Tuesday,
me and Annabel,
and the stumbling bagpipes.

What Dad said

This is what Dad said
when I told him about me and Annabel
wanting to drive and not come back
for a year or so ...

"Son." (When he says *son* I know a story
    is not far behind.)
"Son. When I was eighteen
I'd already decided to ask your Mum to marry me.
And I had my journalism degree half-finished.
I wanted my own desk, my own typewriter,
a home to put them in, and I wanted your Mum.
She said yes, and the rest followed.
At twenty-two, we had this home.
At twenty-two, I learned gardening.
You know the big golden ash in the corner?
I planted that first year here.
Most of our friends were going overseas,
taking winter holiday work in the snow,
or getting drunk every night at the pub.
At twenty-two, your Mum and I
were sitting on the veranda with a cup of cocoa
and a fruit cake.
I'm fifty-two years old this August.
You're a smart kid Jack. A smart kid.

I think you and Annabel should get out of here
as fast as possible. Have a year doing anything
you want. My going-away present is enough money
to buy a car, a cheap old one OK. You'll have to
work somewhere to buy the petrol, and to keep going.
But go."

Let me tell you
it wasn't what I expected.

But maybe, just maybe,
I understand the old man more now.
More than I ever have.

*F*or once in my life

When Jack told me last night
about leaving
what I really wanted to say
was *NO*.
Like a father should.
NO.
And I had all the words ready,
all the clichés loaded
but I couldn't do it.
He looked so hungry,
so much in need of going
that I gave him my first big speech in years,
only this time it was one he wanted to hear.
So that's it.

When Jack was asleep last night
I went into his room.
I sat beside his bed
        and listened to his breathing.
I don't know for how long.
I listened,
and with each breath
I felt his yearning, and confidence,
and strength.
I walked out of his room
sure I'd said the right thing

maybe not as a father
but as a Dad.
I'd said the right thing,
for once in my life.

A *1974 Corona*

It's a 1974 Corona sedan
that's been driven by a
middle-aged single bank manager
called Wilbur who never went out on the weekend
except for a Sunday morning drive with his Mum
to church five kilometres down the road
and enjoyed cleaning it's dull brown duco
every Saturday instead of
    watching the football
    getting drunk
    doing overtime
    or playing with snappy children.

All I had to do was give him $1200
and a handshake to drive it home,
through a mudpuddle or two,
and take that crucifix off the mirror,
give it to the kid next door,
and maybe even consider a paint job ...

but no, let's leave it brown.
Bank manager brown.
That's my car.
That's my ticket with Annabel, out of here.

Annabel on Jack

Jack reads too many books.
He thinks we're going to drive all year
and have great adventures.
He thinks the little money
we have will last.
He wants to sleep in the car,
cook dinner over an open fire.
I'm just waiting for him to
pack a fishing line, smiling,
saying "we can live off the land".
Jesus Christ.
I'm not gutting a fish and cooking it.
But
I do want to go,
even if it only lasts a month or two.
Even if we drive to Melbourne and back
and don't talk to another person.
I want to go.
Why?
Because I've never
been more than 200 kilometres from home,
and that was with my parents, on holiday.
And because Jack's smart,
but not that smart, if you know what I mean.
You watch.
First week, we'll be out of money,

sleeping near a smelly river,
eating cold baked beans out of a can.
The car will have a flat battery
and Jack will be saying something like,
"Isn't this great. Back to nature.
Living off the land. Not a care in the world."
Jesus Christ.

Jack driving

I love to drive,
to blast back to boyhood
where I dreamt of a highway,
a car with a floor-shift
and nowhere to sleep for a week,
burning rubber and a dare
to take every bend
faster than advised.
Even now
I think of a blow-out
as a test for how steady
my hands are on the wheel,
my knuckles white with impatience.
Me, Annabel and
the stereo sing,
trucks threaten our dreams
like thunder,
as we reach the hill
curse the oncoming lights,
I strain to keep the revs up
as we crest the rise,
I snap into top
glide down the mountain
escape ramp 500 metres ahead,
we don't need it.

*T*wo days out

Two days out.
Last night we slept in the car.
Yes, by a river, as I predicted.
Not smelly though.
Clean. Surprisingly clean.
Jack and I had a bath in it.
A naked goose pimple bath.
We raced each other from bank to bank.
We even used soap.
My Mum's going-away present.
Soap-on-a-rope. It floats!

We lay on the grass.
The sun dried our white bodies.
We did nothing for as long as possible.

In the quiet afternoon
we drove for hours.
Jack said, "I'm hungry"
and the bloody car slowed to a stop.
Jack looking at me,
me at Jack,
and neither of us knowing why.
Then I looked at the petrol gauge.
Empty.

Empty, and food, cold river baths
and the nearest town
were all a million miles away.
Two days out ...

As I stood on the lonely backroad,
I'm sure I heard birds,
kookaburras,
laughing ...

*T*he ride

"You two heading anywhere special?"
he says, changing down gear, double-clutching
and churning the old truck's insides loud.
Annabel and I look at each other.
What's this mean?
I decide to answer a question with a question.
I learnt that in Year 9
and it hasn't failed me yet.
"Why?"

"Why. Because I got fifty acres of ripe apples
and a town full of unemployed kids that
hate the sight of them, that's why.
And my kids and I can't pick fifty acres
in two years, much less two months.
I'll pay you, give you a place to sleep.
That's if you're interested?"

The truck cabin rattles over potholes.
He winds down the window
and flicks his cigarette out.

It's not what I'm expecting.
Two days away, out of petrol, and offered a job.
I wanted to get as far as possible,
not a few hundred kilometres down the road.

But it's money. And a place to stay.
Annabel squeezes my hand and I know
it's a *yes* squeeze.
I squeeze back and before I can answer
Annabel says,
'Sure mister. We'll take it. I like apples."

George smiles and says,
"You'll be picking Miss, not eating them."

But he's all right.
Anyone who drives a truck this old can't be too bad.

This Quiet Land

*H*aybales

It was from a book I read in school.
Two teenagers and a shed full
　　of stacked haybales,
a crow's nest in the loft,
and her father, the farmer, in town.
I can't remember anything else but
these two, barely fifteen years old,
lying up high on the bales
and the boy with his hand
　　up her dress,
and they're both shaking,
even though it's summer outside.
She takes off her dress,
her bra, and undies,
stands on the highest bale
and gestures him up.
And in a tumble of straw and clothes
they made nervous love
page after page.
First from his side,
　　all awkward, lopsided, and flush.
Then hers,
　　sweat and itch and eyes on the crow's nest.
I kept that book for years.
And when George offered us his shed to sleep in,
I said *yes*,
and asked if it had haybales …

The farm

The road goes through a path of pines.
It's dusty and hot, but here, for a while,
the trees hold the cool and dark,
then a sharp left and you see the wooden house,
surrounded by wattles and a sagging fence.
Two kids run out,
no more than ten years old,
both jump on the tray while the truck's still moving,
country kids.
There's someone else, older,
sixteen maybe, a girl,
standing in the dirt of the drive,
wearing overalls and dusty riding boots,
and when we turn to park near the shed,
I see she's pregnant.
George says, "that's Emma, my eldest",
as the four dogs start barking all at once,
sniffing our hands and boots,
and running around George, jumping up,
and not stopping barking,
not for a second.

Craig

I'm Craig. I'm ten next week.
You come to pick apples for us?
You gunna stay? Lots don't stay,
reckon it's too hard.
Reckon Dad don't pay enough.
Reckon we're stupid to live this far from town.
You gunna stay?
We need help, Dad says.
Now Emma can't pick.
She's pregnant you know.
Gunna have twins, or three, or four.
She's so big. Bigger than a cow.
Bigger than a house.
She couldn't climb the ladder to pick now.
You ever picked before?
I can pick two bins a day.
I reckon it's good for football training.
You two married?
You're not gunna get pregnant are you?
Anyway, I'll see ya.
My sister's name is Beck, she's seven.
She don't talk much.
Not like me.
See ya.

*T*his quiet land

It's nothing more than an irrigation channel
dug across the plains,
but George, despite his eye on the harvest
    and it's price,
years before built a hardwood landing
to dive off into the cool water.
Annabel and I spend every afternoon
    after picking
lying on the wet timber
    listening to the frogs
and watching the dragonflies skim across the surface.

What can I say?
When we know George is in town
    or too busy hosing down the tractor
we strip naked and worship the late breeze
blowing ripples across the channel.
A beer or two and I'm set for life.
A beer or two and Annabel's lips
    and her arm resting on my stomach
    and I hope to never leave
the late afternoon
    of tired muscles, channel water,
    and this quiet land.

*T*he shed

Me and Annabel are sitting against the shed.
In the sun.
Sunday. No work.
I'm dreaming of a month of Sundays.
We've been working for two weeks.
Our hands are starting to heal
        from the first week of learning
        to snap the stem of each apple
        as we plucked it.
        Yes, "pluck", that's what George says.
George loves his apples so much
        he can't bear to just pick them.
        He plucks them quick, yet soft,
        places them in his bag
        and when it's full
        leans over the bin and releases the latch.
He fills four, sometimes five bins a day.
That first week Annabel and I averaged three together,
from 7am to 5pm. Climbing ladders with the bag
half-full,
swinging in front, pulling your neck forward.
I cursed my luck for running out of petrol.

The second week was easier.
George gave us the heavy trees, loaded down,
until the weight broke the branches.

We filled four bins a day. By Friday, it was five.
Twenty Dollars a bin.
George says we're all right.
So "alright" last night he came into the shed
with a dozen bottles of beer.

I like the sun when I'm tired.
I lay down,
close my eyes and think of
anything but apples.

*C*raig on his Mum

Mum ran away from us
the night Beck vomited all over the dinner.
She didn't take much,
except the blind cat and all our money.
Well, that's what Dad said.
Beck vomited all over everyone's dinner.
It was unreal. I don't know if that's why Mum left,
but she left,
and for weeks I kept thinking she was hiding
somewhere on the farm,
in the shed,
or camping down by the channel,
and I kept hoping she'd just
come walking back into the kitchen,
but that hasn't happened.

I'm learning to cook now.
So is Beck.
We get our own breakfast and lunch,
and sometimes we cook dinner —
you know, spaghetti and some sauce,
from a jar.
Emma can cook, pretty good too.
I miss Mum sometimes,
and I know Beck does too,
but Beck hasn't vomited since.

Not at the dinner table or anywhere,
and Mum might come back one day.
Dad says she won't.
He doesn't say much about her,
which is funny because they
must have been pretty friendly,
don't you reckon,
to get married and all.

I'm not getting married.
I'm not having kids who vomit all over the dinner.
But I might run away from here,
when I'm older.
I might even go look for Mum.

*M*y Dad says ...

My Dad says you're good workers.
He says you're the best he's had in years.
He says he doesn't care what you do in our shed,
as long as you keep working the same.
He said that last night at dinner.
I asked him what you do in our shed,
and Emma laughed.
She hasn't laughed in a while
and then she says,
"Yeah Dad, tell Craig what they're doing."
But Dad doesn't.
He tells Beck not to eat so fast,
probably scared of her vomiting again.
He tells me to mind my own business,
but Dad tells me that at least once a day,
so it's nothing new.
And that's why I'm here now.
So you tell me, OK,
what do you do in our shed here?

*B*eck talks

My brother Craig,
he thinks he knows everything,
but
he doesn't know who let the dog
wee in his football boots …

I know.

Screwed

Screwed

I got screwed.
That's how I got pregnant.
Screwed.
If you want to know, I'll tell you.
The truth.
Not what I told Dad.
"My boyfriend, Dad."
The one I made up.
The one who had to leave town with his parents
on account of his father's work.
What a load of bull.
What boyfriend.
We live twenty kilometres from town.
The school bus is our only link.
School buses don't take you anywhere after 3pm.
So one Friday I arranged to stay
at my friend Jenny's place.
The Friday her parents are away,
and we have a party.
All of Year 10.
A big party. A loud party.
And I drink too much,
even dance a bit, just to show myself I can.
I'm drinking away
the twenty kilometres of loneliness out here.
I'm drinking away

the exam results that don't take me anywhere.
I'm drinking away
my clothes that smell of this farm.
I'm drinking away
apples, apple pie, baked apples, apple juice,
apple jam for God's sake.
Then I pass out,
feeling pretty good really.

I passed out on Jenny's lounge.
In the morning I woke on her parent's bed,
with no clothes on.

I got screwed.
I got pregnant.
And I didn't even get to enjoy
becoming this big and ugly.
And nobody in Year 10 knows a thing.
Nobody, that is,
except one person.

School photos

I've been going through my school photos.
Every one since Year 5.
I'm making a list of each boy's features.
Big nose, blond hair, freckles, ears that stick out.
I've got twenty-one boys from Year 10
going back for years.
What a bunch of uglies,
and watching them get uglier every year
are all my girlfriends.
The girls who didn't see anything at Jenny's party.
None of them wear glasses,
so maybe they were just blind drunk.
Blind drunk. Or too scared to remember anything.
Twenty-one boys. Twenty-one prospective fathers.
Ten with blond hair.
Ten with dark hair.
And nerdy Phillip Montain with
red hair, freckles, and … surely not!

It may take years of comparing their features
with that of my baby,
but when I do,
and I know,
well,
someone's going to get screwed,
and, this time,
it won't be me.

Colours

It's the sky I love.
Annabel and I sunbathe
on the hardwood landing of the channel.
I spend hours lost
in the deep summer blue
that goes forever.
I remember being a kid,
me and Dad climbing
onto our roof and looking up.
I'd dream we were flying
and all summer
I'd never want to land.
Annabel and I imagine
animals in the clouds, like kids do,
as a distant jet
writes across the sky
longer than history
and I lay back
remember being a kid again
lost in the innocent colours
of childhood.

Annabel and babies

I think about babies.
My baby, when and if.
Emma's baby, twenty kilometres from town,
no Dad, but lots of apple mush for food.
Jack and me with a baby.
I'm not serious,
I'm just thinking,
passing this Saturday while Jack works
on our car that goes nowhere, but goes nowhere well.
When I left school and got into Uni
I thought my life was made.
Uni, job, money, Jack, travel, house,
Jack, more travel,
and still Jack.
Jack was the constant.

Then one weekend he says
he's quitting.
He wants to drive, anywhere,
as long as it's away from Uni and home.
He wants me to come.
That night my room seemed so small
like a kids room, full of toys and stuff
and none of it meant anything.
I picked up my textbooks
and tried reading them,

and I realised for five years
I'd been reading books that didn't make sense,
and now, I had four more years of it.

I went downstairs and told Mum and Dad.
It's one Sunday they won't forget.
Dad raved, Mum cried.
Then Dad asked *why?*
And all I could answer was
     because I'm too young to decorate a home
     because text books have really bad covers
     because I don't want to wear neat clothes
       and wake every morning at 7.30
     because Jack and I have never been wrong yet
and because I want a year for myself, not my future.

So, late Sunday, we did a deal.
My Dad, the solicitor, bargained
a year off, a deferment,
then back to the books.
I agreed. What else could I do?
And now,
I'm thinking about babies.
Emma's baby.
Jack and my baby.
Growing in my mind, if not in my womb.

*T*he dew-wet grass

The best time is early morning
with the dew-wet grass,
the hills shouldered in mist,
everything quiet.
Annabel and I climb each ladder,
pick a cold apple
and crunch away.
The juice so sharp and tart
it hurts my teeth.
We sit like this,
watching the crows in the fir trees,
the silver-eyes darting among the fruit,
listening for George's tractor
with the empty bins rattling,
calling to be filled.
Annabel, the mist, a farm apple, the birds,
and an orchard waking up.

*L*ucky Emma

Sometimes
I feel like someone
who's won the smallest prize in the lottery
but lost the ticket.
I think of all the Year 10 boys.
Mark Spencer with his long hair,
black silverchair T-shirt,
leaning back in his chair
playing air-guitar all through Maths.
Peter Borovski and his love affair with himself.
>   "Hey Peter, who you sleeping with tonight?
>   You're kidding. Yourself again.
>   What I'd give for your luck.
>   And confidence. And stupidity."
Luke Banfield, who once this year talked to a girl,
yeah, once. He asked her if she'd seen his basketball.
I was that lucky girl.
Or maybe, just maybe,
Steve Dimitri, one of the few fifteen year olds I know
who can eat with his mouth closed
who doesn't know how to play basketball
who doesn't look at the ground when talking to a girl
and who doesn't vomit after three drinks.
He vomits after five drinks …

Actually, I take back what I said.
I feel like someone
who's won the smallest prize in the lottery,
found the ticket
and has to collect the winnings
even though
she doesn't want them.

*E*mma

I wish I had a boyfriend like you.
Someone who wanted to be with me,
all the time.
It's true.
I watch you two in the orchard.
Every ten minutes he stops picking
to look where you are.
Sometimes you see him, sometimes not,
but he's there, checking you out.
He's not my physical type mind,
but,
I'd love to have someone like that.
And someone to sleep with.
What's that like?
Every night. Does he hold you?
Does he snore?
Does he kiss you before sleep?
God! I've been watching too many soap operas,
but I'd like to know.
The only person I've slept with
is bloody Craig when he was scared one night.
He spent all night dropping silent bombers
under the blankets. What a brother!
Yeah, I'd like a boyfriend,
but I don't like my chances at the moment.
You're a lucky girl,
you know that.

Annabel

It hurt,
listening to Emma talk like that.
It's like some bad dream,
pregnant,
and she didn't even have sex,
well, not really.
It's not the Immaculate Conception though.

I like her.
She's upfront.
She's taking it better than I would.
I'd buy a gun and shoot all twenty-one boys, on suspicion.
And then Jack and I come along,
making love every night in her shed,
and she notices stuff, about Jack.
I've stopped noticing.
She makes me grateful.
I'm going to drive into town later
and buy Jack something,
a CD, or a new shirt maybe.
I might buy Emma
a dress, normal-size,
for after the baby.
A new dress to show the world
on her one trip to town every month.
Her one trip to town, for groceries.

*E*mma and her Mum

Mum and I were cooking
the Sunday before she left.
She stopped blending, and sifting,
she looked out the window
at the day
and I remember it was hot
with not a breath of wind.
Craig and Beck were outside
fighting over whose turn it was
to ride the bike.
Mum looked out, past them,
past the sagging fence,
and the tree-line,
and she said,
"A farm takes a lot out of you,
   sometimes too much."
I thought she was just complaining,
or dreaming,
so I didn't question her.
And that night
Beck vomited all over the Sunday dinner.
That was our last meal together.

When I think of Mum and what she did
I get stiff in this chair
and I look out the same window,

past the same fence, over the same tree-line,
and I touch my stomach
and I whisper,
"I won't ever leave you
  I won't ever ..."

Lucky

George thinks we're mad.
Emma thinks we're mad.
Craig and Beck think it's cool
sleeping on a bed of haybales
five metres from the ground
a thin foam mattress
to cover the hay
and blankets, lots of them
piled up high.
Annabel and I climb
the haybale stairs
and feel like King and Queen.
Sometimes we hear the possums
scurrying across the roof
and the birds nesting
in the rusted gutters
and late at night
when the farm sleeps
I hear Annabel's breathing,
a distant owl, and the
slow rhythm of the
windvane on the farmhouse roof.
George and Emma are wrong.
We're not mad, we're lucky.

George

George talks about the weather,
he talks about apples,
sometimes, when he's in a good mood,
he talks about his kids.
This is one of those times.
Lunch in the orchard.
Packed sandwiches and a thermos of tea.
Annabel and I sit against the tractor.
George squats in the shade of a tree
and talks,
"Good kids, all of them.
Sure Craig never shuts up,
but what ten-year-old does?
And he's strong.
He helps out around the place.
He'll try and lift anything.
Poor kid will have a hernia before he's a teenager!
And Beck's sweet. She always calls me Dadda.
And I feel like a real Dad when I read to her at night.
She won't sleep without one story, at least.
She's quiet, like me, but smarter.
And Emma, angry with the world.
You can see it, can't you?
But then, she's got reason to be."

George's voice trails off.
We both keep quiet.
He'll tell us if he wants.
"When she first told me,
I wanted to get my gun.
Yeah, I know,
just what you'd expect from a father.
And I would have,
if her mother was around.
I would have made a big show of being angry,
shouted, stormed around looking for bullets,
vowing to chase the kid out of town.
But without Emma's mother here
it seemed pointless.
So I sat and talked, and listened too.
I'm glad I did.
She dismissed the boy, whoever it was.
Someone who's left town.
Some boyfriend I never knew.
You know, I'm still not sure
if she's telling me the truth,
or if she's protecting somebody,
but, it doesn't matter.
What matters is the kid.
I keep telling myself that.
I don't think of becoming a grandad.

I just think of my little girl
becoming a Mum.
Sometimes I wish her mother was here,
for the baby. For Emma.
Not for me.
Emma's mother is dead for me.
She died the day she left."

George looks at us,
as if he's just noticed we're here.
I'm sure he'd been working all that stuff
through these last few months,
here in the orchard,
and it's finally out.

"I talk too much.
She's not dead.
But I'm glad of one thing.
When she left, I'm glad she took her clothes,
her jewellery, even most of the money,
and, by Christ,
I'm glad she left me the kids.
I'd be lost without them.
Lost and bitter.
With them here, I'm only bitter."

George gets up,
tips the tea out under a tree,
packs the esky with what's left
and says,
"Come on, the apples won't pick themselves.
You two are good workers.
I hope you'll stay for the season.
You'll see Emma's baby too, maybe.
By the way, have you ever seen a baby being born?"

Now that was something for Annabel and me
to think of all afternoon.

*L*ike a drunk ...

The night of the day
George told us about seeing the baby
Annabel and I got drunk.
We sat on our favourite haybales
and drank beer, cold and bitter
straight from the bottle.
As the evening light dimmed
we climbed into our makeshift bed
and made noisy love,
like farm animals in the barn
like a drunk falling into a pub, penniless
like a bird caught in the crosshair of a gun
like a truck with no brakes, half-way down a hill
like a kid with a match and a paddock of dry grass
like George without a wife
like Emma without a lover
like a baby, crying to be born.

*E*mma and the memory

Sometimes,
I think I can feel it happening.
I mean,
I can remember how it felt.
It wasn't the pain,
not real pain, like when you cut your hand,
or tread on a rusty nail, or anything,
more an irritation,
a dull irritation,
pressing on me.
And I can smell it too,
like dirty socks left in the laundry basket too long,
and stale beer, but that was probably me.
And I can taste salt, my own tears?
I wasn't crying surely? I was passed out!
Maybe he was crying, the bastard.
I hope he was. Crying with shame.
The only woman he could get was unconscious.
The thought gives me pleasure, at least.
That's all.
I lie in bed, thinking of how it felt.
Not knowing if it's my imagination,
or suppressed memory,
or what really happened.

I remember waking up.
I walked into Jenny's bathroom and vomited.
Only then did I realise I was naked.
Naked, sore, wet, sticky,
and slowly becoming
very, very
suspicious.

*S*taying at school

Dad says I should have stayed at school,
should have kept going right up to the day.
Now wouldn't that be a sight,
me in a school uniform.
Size 18 wouldn't even fit this belly.
And Personal Development classes
would have had special meaning, don't you think.
Me, six months pregnant,
learning about the correct use of condoms
and other devices,
and you know what I would have said
to that Mrs Barber, our teacher,
as she was showing us condoms on carrots?
I would have put my hand up right there,
and said,
"Miss, how do you keep from getting pregnant
    when you're passed out drunk
    and someone takes advantage?"
It would almost be worth going back to school
just to ask that one question ...

*E*mma's dream

Sometimes, when I'm asleep,
I have a dream where
I'm living in a city,
going to work in fancy clothes,
and I have a boyfriend,
and a house of my own
on a normal city street,
you know,
with neighbours, and a shop down the road,
and the only animal is a pet dog,
and the only trees are for shade,
or flowers, or decoration.
In this dream
I go out to the movies
with my boyfriend
and we eat dinner
in a restaurant,
and on weekends I don't have to do anything
but enjoy myself.
And in this dream
I'm walking to work on Monday
and I'm nearly there,
and I remember the baby,
my baby,
and it gets kind of strange
in my dream

because I'm standing outside my work
trying to remember
if I have a baby
or not,
and where it is,
and that's when
I'm not sure
if my dream
is a dream,
or a nightmare.

Sunday Annabel

Another Sunday of sunshine,
no work, and swimming in the channel.
Emma sits by the bank
watching Jack swing from the rope
and drop into a welcome of still water.
I'm lying here, soaking up a day off,
listening to the sound of nothing
but Jack being a kid again.
Emma talks about school,
and her days on this farm
and how she wants to leave
and every time she mentions leaving
I notice her hands touching her stomach.
I listen and silently vow
to not mention Jack and I leaving
as soon as the work's done.
I tell Emma about where we live
in the suburbs
and the sounds we hear
and the neighbours,
and how Jack and I
just had to get out,
to end up here.
Emma looks up quick when I say this,
and I know what she's thinking.
She knows we can leave when we want.

At that moment Jack falls between us
and starts shaking the water off himself,
like a mad dog,
looking for some attention.

*R*ich, smart, or stupid

You must be rich, smart,
or real stupid you two.
That's what Emma says.
She says only way you could be doing this
is to be rich, smart, or stupid.
She says most people would have to stay home,
study, or work, or have babies maybe.
She says you two get to drive around the place,
work when you want —
she thinks that makes you smart.
And you don't worry about money.
You buy beer whenever,
you buy each other presents,
you go into town and eat —
she thinks that makes you rich.
She says you're rich and smart
but
she says
you're staying here by choice
when you could drive away.
You're staying here working in the orchard,
and sleeping in a shed.
She says that makes you stupid.

A Place Like This

*A*nnabel dreams

It comes in the late afternoon.
I'm in the orchard,
halfway up the ladder,
my neck aching with the weight of the bag
stretching to reach one full red apple,
and I suddenly think of University.
> The afternoon lecture,
> fifty of us, all dressed in jeans & T-shirts
> taking notes
> searching for the phrase that will guarantee
> good exam results.
> Pages and pages,
> and I'd stop for a second
> to touch my forehead.
> I'd feel the small furrow
> between my eyes,
> deepening, it seems,
> with every afternoon lecture.
I sit on the ladder,
rest the bag on the lower rung
hold that apple, rub it along my cheek,
my forehead, smoothing away my past,
and I take long slow crunching bites
as the afternoon breeze

wakens the silver-eyes in the branches,
and I spend all my education
on doing nothing but eating and watching
for just long enough
to feel clean again.

*J*ack

We came here for the money.
George happened along at the right time.
We had no petrol, nowhere to stay,
and no plans.
When I think about it we had to say yes.
It was that, or go home,
with nothing.
I keep feeling I owe George,
and his children.
I know about the quiet revolution
in every family.
I think of my sister and me eight years ago,
waiting, knowing our Mum was going to die.
Knowing, even at our age.
It took me years to work out what to think,
where to put that stuff.
And I look at Emma here,
and George, the strain in his eyes,
and his voice.
I know where it's coming from
and it won't go away, not for awhile.
I'm glad we came here.
I work extra hard in the orchard,
not for the money anymore,
but for something I can't explain.
Something worth more than money.

*T*he Department lady

I got a visitor from town yesterday,
the Department lady.
Talking about after the baby's born.
What I can get to help.
Money? Not enough.
Health Care. "Don't worry, he won't get sick," I said.
And New Mothers' Monday meeting
where everyone talks about
how beautiful their baby is.
I put a stop to that one.
I asked her if the Department would give me a car,
you know,
to make the meeting on time.
Then she asked me about school.
If I wanted to go back.
I could get money.
I could get my Leaving Certificate.

I wanted to ask her about it,
but she was such a cow.

She started packing up.
Her visit over. The government's job done.
And I didn't like her.
The way she looked at the old lino in the kitchen,
and the dirty dishes,

and she never looked me in the eye,
she looked at her paperwork,
then at our cheap living,
and she asked too many questions.

So when she said goodbye,
I said there was one thing she could do,
I looked at her straight,
the way I'm looking at you now,
and I said,
"You could find out who the father is,
   that'd be a big help ..."

She didn't have an answer for that.
People like her only ever have questions.

*A*nnabel on love

Mine was Year 10.
Jack.
After the movies, at my doorstep,
like a stupid Romance novel.
He kissed me. Nice, but quick.
From my bedroom window
I saw him walking home
and I wanted more.
More was months later.

What can I say?
It's embarrassing now to remember.
He felt heavy and awkward,
lying on top of me.
I'm trying to kiss him,
but his mind's elsewhere.
He's trying to put it in,
and he can't,
so I reached down
and did it for him, simple.

And do you know what was the best bit?
Afterwards.
When he lay in me, limp,
and we held each other,
and started kissing again,

slow and soft, no pressure,
and we started giggling
and kissing still
and touching each other,
relieved it was over,
so now we could start
to really make love,

and we haven't stopped.

Emma replies

In Year 9 I kissed a boy,
after school.
Netball training cancelled,
and me alone, shooting hoops,
with an hour to spare, waiting for Dad.
And Rick Harvey comes over,
starts shooting with me.
Offers me a game of keyring,
twenty cents a basket,
and he wins a few,
I win a few.
He owes me forty cents,
when I know he's got no money
or no desire to give me money,
but he's all right
and we sit against the clubhouse
close enough,
and he leans over and starts kissing me.
No questions, no waiting,
and it's OK
so I kiss back.
For a while we just sit there,
our lips pressing,
then I feel his hand
on my leg
tracing a path up

and he's soft and gentle really
so I let him touch me,
you know, there,
outside my pants,
then inside,
and he's not pushy or anything,
and we're both very quiet now,
we've stopped kissing really,
our lips are just together,
our minds are down below, up my dress,
and he puts his finger inside me
and I like it,
and he keeps touching me
inside and out
and soon all I'm thinking of is my body.
I'm hardly sure he's there,
it's me and my body
and I don't move a muscle
in case it all stops
and he keeps doing the same thing
for minutes, for hours
for God knows.
I loved it.
I tell you
it was Christmas, and Easter,
and chocolate cake, and dreams,

and birthdays
and it wasn't Rick Harvey

it was me.
Me and my body,
waking up.

*H*e asks

A funny thing happened today.
In town.
I was in Penney's Department store,
looking at baby clothes,
but daydreaming really.
Thinking how am I going to learn
to be a good mum.
You know, stuff like what to feed him,
or her,
what to do if they look sick,
or hot, or cold, or they cry too much.
I'm thinking all this
as I look through the baby clothes I can't afford
when someone behind me says hello.
It's Adam Barlow, from school. Year 10.
He's in his uniform,
shirt hanging out as usual
socks down, bunched over his sneakers.
He looks nervous,
here in the baby section of Penney's.
He asks how I've been.
He asks how long before the baby's born.
He asks what it's like on the farm
        with no school to worry.
He asks if I know what I'll call it.
He asks what my Dad thinks.

He asks if I'll come back to school afterwards.
He asks again how I've been.
Then he says he's got to go.
He asks far too many questions,
and he answers none.

A gentle kick

As Adam Barlow
walked out of Penney's yesterday
I felt my baby kick.
A gentle tap really,
as if my child
was reminding me
of what's important
and what's not
as Adam Barlow
walked out.

*J*ack's plans

This is not what I planned.
I wanted lonely beaches with Annabel
and bush camping
beside a river
and maybe even time in the snow
working for a season
amongst the wealthy.
Not here,
jump-starting tractors
sleeping in a shed
working ten-hour days
and now, get this,
going to birth classes
with Emma and Annabel!
I'm eighteen years old
and going to birth classes
for a girl who's not my girlfriend
for a baby that's not mine
and I've got to admit
yes
when I think about it
I've got to admit
I'm looking forward to it!

Emma deserves help,
like George needed help with picking.

And one day,
maybe one day,
Annabel and I will want a baby.
God!
I'm starting to sound like my Dad.
Birth classes.
God!
I hope I don't have to touch anything.
Or lay on my back and breathe funny …

*U*ncle Craig

I hope Emma has the baby at home.
I want to see it,
you know,
being born.
I've seen calves, and lambs,
and even a piglet being born,
but never a real baby.
I reckon it'll be unreal.
Emma says after I was born
I cried for days.
She said I'd never shut up
which is funny really
because Dad says I never shut up now
so maybe that's what happens,
you get born and act the same
your whole life.
Anyway, I'm being real nice to Emma now,
so she'll let me watch
and you know
it means I'll be an uncle,
at my age.
It'll be unreal.

Different

You two are different.
Different than my school friends.
They want to know about the baby, sure,
but only because they're not pregnant
and only because they've got nothing else to say,
not since Jenny's party anyway.
They don't want to know about me.
And how it feels
    to be carrying this great weight
    to be a mother without a boyfriend
    to be missing school, and parties,
    and all of my friends.

I'm glad you're here.
I'm glad you're coming with me to my classes.
I couldn't go alone,
and I need to know stuff
    about the birth.
Truth is, I'm scared.
I'm sure Dad's truck won't start.
Or the ambulance won't come.
Or the midwife.
Or I'll be home alone
with everyone in the orchard.
And the pain,
and how long it'll take.

It's kind of funny really.
Jenny, Peter, Rick Harvey,
even Adam bloody Barlow
are hard at it studying
for their exams
and I'm here
about to study
for something much bigger …
I hope I pass.

Saturday night

The drunk night.
George in town.
The farmhouse asleep.
Annabel and me on the haybales,
stacked high.
We can almost touch the roof.
A bottle of wine,
a dozen beers,
and all night.
Drinking and telling stories,
like
your first embarrassing moment,
the day you learnt Santa wasn't real,
the first time you vomited,
the day you learnt your parents
      did more than just sleep together,
and the first time you got drunk.

Hours of stories,
here, above the farm
on our haybales.

At midnight
Annabel took off all her clothes
      without saying a word,

then asked for another glass of beer, please.
So beautiful, and so well-mannered.

What could I do?
I took a long drink
and undressed.
Annabel cheered
as we stood,
straining to touch the roof,
from our naked haybale world.

*T*he snake

It was two metres long,
brown and mean,
and coming after the chickens.
I nearly stepped on the thing,
and, yes, it was probably as scared as me,
but I jumped higher,
and I picked up the shovel leaning against the shed
and hit it hard,
once, right in the middle,
and again on it's head,
and again and again,
until I was sure,
and again because I'd never be sure,
and then I felt sick
and I ran behind the shed to vomit.
Nothing but green bile came up,
green bile and tears.

I walked back
and George was inspecting it.
A King Brown.
Annabel came out and saw it too.
And Craig. And Beck.
The farm dogs still barked at it,

too late now to be of any use.
Everyone standing out in the sun
looking at the snake,
except Annabel,
who's looking at me.

Annabel's snake

All night, in the shed,
I held Jack.
He was sweating in the chill air,
waking every hour, jerking his legs,
as if running.
I held his arms, tight.
I could feel the muscles tense,
wanting to move,
wanting to flex,
so I held him.
I didn't sleep much, maybe an hour.
Most of the night,
I watched Jack
strike that snake
a thousand times over
and not once, in his sleep,
did that snake die.

*B*eck's snake

After it was all over
I picked it up
took it down to the garden
and I buried it
deep in the ground
where it's quiet
where it's safe
where the dogs can't get it.

Naming rights

I'm going to call him Joseph,
or Josephine if it's a girl.
Why?
Because it's a strong name,
Joe, Joseph.
You give a kid a name like Cameron
or Alfred, or something like that,
and they end up wearing glasses
and looking at computers for the rest of their life.
And Matthew and Nathan
enter school with another
fifteen Matthews and Nathans beside them.
So Joe it is.
He'll turn out strong. Strong and smart.
And I thought of Joseph, you know,
in the Bible.
Him and Mary and Immaculate Conception.
Well, I reckon my baby's conception
was pretty damn immaculate.
And I couldn't call the kid Jesus,
could I?
Joseph.
Josephine.

Cheers

It's six weeks since we left home.
Our great adventure ran out of petrol
and stopped on this farm.
The harvest is nearly done.
George looks happier,
he lets me drive the tractor,
he lets us finish early on Friday.
He even let Emma come to town with us last Saturday.
We watched the local football.
Big farmers tackling even bigger truckies
and their sons, stepping effortlessly
around them all.
A few of Emma's friends came up to say hello.
They all asked the same questions.
Baby this, baby that.
Emma only existed as the baby-carrier it seems.
They all looked slightly guilty,
especially the girls,
as though a bond had been broken,
or something, I don't know.
We sat on the bonnet of our car
and clapped
when someone scored a try,
and we all cheered whenever
Adam Barlow got tackled.
Emma, Annabel, and I
cheered the game,
and cheered ourselves.

*E*mma and apples

I needed to get away from the farm,
if only for a day.
People say apples have no smell,
well, even now,
twenty kilometres away,
I can still smell them.
I'll smell them when I'm dead, I reckon.
If you stay too long on the farm
you'll get the same, for sure.
It's alright for Craig.
He wants to be a farmer,
he's got apple juice for blood.
And Beck? She'll escape
on her brains, I bet.
But me? Where do I fit?
Not on the farm,
not in a one-pub town
like this,
not anywhere I guess.
Maybe in a city,
where I can get lost,
get lost for good.

*E*_{mma}

After the football on Saturday,
when Jack, Annabel and me
got back into the car,
I had this urge to drive and not stop,
to tell Jack to just keep going,
to follow the Midland Highway forever,
just the three of us.
I've had enough of this town,
and my friends
asking guilty stupid questions,
and I've had enough
of the smell of our farm
and the animals' noise,
and the winter winds whipping down Broken Lookout
and rattling our house.
I wanted to forget being pregnant
and remember being young,
like Jack and Annabel are with each other.

I was thinking all this on Saturday
in the car
when we reached Broken Lookout
where Jack parked, for the view,
and Annabel said,
"There's the farm.
It looks so beautiful at night."

Jack agreed,
and I looked at the stars,
the thousands of stars in the cold sky,
but I couldn't say a single word.

Craig hates school

I hate school.
I hate school.
I hate the kids in Year 8 and 9
who come up to me at lunch
and ask "hey, where's fat Emma.
Where's your sister, we want to try our luck."
I hate school
I can't fight the big kids,
but I do anyway.
I get one good kick, or punch,
before they clobber me,
or the teachers come.
The sooner Emma has a baby, the better.
I hate school.

A *place like this*

I go walking, early.
Me and my baby.
Me and my big stomach.
We walk to the channel
sit on the bank
watch the dragonflies
like mad helicopters cutting the surface.
I go walking
to avoid the kitchen
and the smell of food,
too early for cooking,
Craig and Beck arguing,
and Dad looking out the window,
thinking of money.
I go walking to watch the trees
and the sun's light filtering through them.
I talk to my baby.
I describe the farm.
I tell him about the apples
and the blossoms in spring
and the Paterson's Curse that covers the hills
and the birds gorging on rotten fruit.
I tell him everything
as we walk.
Maybe so he won't be disappointed
being born into
a place like this.

Weird

Weird

It's weird.
Very weird.
I started going to birth classes
with Emma and Jack.
I sat in the room, on the floor,
beside them.
Ten couples and the three of us.
Eleven couples holding hands, and me,
not knowing whether to touch Emma or Jack.
And Jack's weird,
he looks at me when he talks to Emma
and looks away.
He can't focus.
He's not sure who he's partner to.
He wants to help Emma I know,
so do I.
But I can't help there.
I can't be her partner,
neither can Jack,
not with me around.
So I keep away.
I stay here in the shed.
I think about Emma's baby,
and Jack.
And where Jack and I are going,

which is nowhere it seems,
and it's all too weird,
too weird to work out.

Craig and the cows

Hey, you know what?
Some Year 9 kids have painted the cows.
Farmer Austin's best dairy cows.
Each cow has a red number on its side.
Some even have sponsors!
One's sponsored by Nike!
Number 23. The Shane Warne of dairy cows!
It's all round school.
It's all round town.
There's even a photo in the newspaper,
old man Austin shaking his head,
looking at his stupid cows.
Everyone at school reckons he should
leave it on, and call them by number,
> "Number 12, your turn for milking."
> "Number 8, stop scratching against the gum tree."
Our footy coach says we should adopt one,
as a mascot.
He says we play like a bunch of cows anyway.
It's great.
The town hasn't been so happy in years.
It's great.
All over a herd of painted cows!

Annabel is ready

I'm ready.
The work is nearly done.
I want to move.
I can almost smell the road
and hear the soft hum of tyres
rolling through this year
where Jack and I plan nothing.
I'm ready. I know.

But Jack's dreaming.
He sits against the shed
reading the same page of his book
over and over.
He's looking for a reason to go,
or stay.
He walks through the house of his past,
hoping he'll find the right door,
hoping he'll find the key.

It pisses me off.
I want to go and shake him,
shake that house down.
I want to tell him he's in the wrong house,
at the wrong time.
I want to tell him we've built a new one,
with no doors locked,

no keys,
just him and me and open space.

I want to move.
Even if it's back to
sleeping in the car by the highway
with tinned food for dinner.
I don't care.
I'm ready.

*J*ack and the beach

The work is nearly done.
Once the top orchard is stripped,
we're finished.
A week, maybe two.
We've saved enough money
for six months of holiday,
camping on a beach.
I keep thinking of the one
I went to as a kid,
with Mum and Dad kissing on a towel
and my sister at the shop, talking to boys.
I want to do nothing for a long time.
No more apples,
or 7am starts.
Annabel and me.
Open fires, books to read,
bathe in the creek behind the surf,
and enough petrol in the car
to go to town whenever we want.
Annabel and me
at the beach.
And we'll get there,
we will,
after the baby.

Annabel

Jack's mad!
He thinks Emma and the baby
are his responsibility.
Uncle Jack.
Mad Uncle Jack.
He's like some crazy social worker.
Everything he touches he can fix.
I should remind him of the car!
So, what's he going to do?
Help Emma have the baby,
and then what?
Jack can't save the world,
beginning on this farm.
This is Emma's life,
she'll work it out.
Jack's got to leave it,
leave it to Emma,
and George.
They'll work it out.
Of that I'm sure.

My Mother died when I was ten.
The last time we spoke
was late in the afternoon,
after school.
She was in bed, resting,
trying to read,
and it was a beautiful day.
The sun shone right up to her bed
and she told me stories,
as well as she could —
she was heavily drugged for the pain.
And I told stories right back.
Only my stories were ones in the future.
What I planned to do.
Me and Dad and my sister.
I told her
to make her know we'd stay together,
you know, afterwards.
I didn't have a clue
what would really happen,
but I kept talking.
And one story was about grandkids.
About me and a wife and babies.
I did it for her.
I didn't want kids, I was ten years old!
I wanted my Mother, alive, and healthy.

But I made up this story,
and Mum smiled and listened,
she even laughed when I promised her
a football team of grandkids.
Then her laughing turned to coughing
and that awful sound she couldn't break.
I left her to rest.
I kissed her forehead,
the way she kissed me every night, before bed,
and I closed the door.
The sun still shone brightly ...

And that's why I go to birth classes with Emma,
why I feel I can't leave now.
Maybe it doesn't make sense.
It's like a death.
Or a birth.

*A*nnabel and the car

Last night
I got in our car
and drove.
Just me.
No Jack. No Emma.
I drove along Turpentine Road,
up to the quarry.
I parked, turned the radio up loud,
and lay back.

I figured I had two choices.
I could keep driving and not come back.
Jack can have the money, and the beach,
and whatever else he can invent.
I'd leave the car outside his house,
and go back to my life.

My other choice was to say *no* to Jack.
To simply say *no*.
The baby will be born,
with or without him here.
And Emma will be a good mother,
and there's George, and Craig, and quiet Beck.

Lots of children don't have fathers,
or mothers.
Jack should know that,
more than all of us.

Craig

Emma says
her son's not living on a farm
all his life
and he's not picking apples
or praying for rain
or busting a gut fixing things that
can't be fixed
and he's not
wearing the same shoes winter and summer
cause that's all he's got.
And Emma says
if it's a girl
she's not marrying a farmer
or cooking all day
for kids who vomit it all back up
and she's not spending nights
watching TV and dreaming,
or getting pregnant at sixteen
and looking after brothers and sisters
and fathers and family.
Emma says all this
and I'm thinking this baby
better be born soon
because it's got a lot of living to do
and a lot of learning on what
not to do.

Birth classes

Ten farmers in flannelette shirts
and me
sit on our knees in a circle
at the CWA Hall.
Ten farmers' wives lean back
against their husbands.
Emma leans against me.
I hold her hands in mine
and talk quietly,
repeating the Instructor's words.
Sometimes I add my own.
Silly stuff like
"she'll write books
 she'll call you Mum, and me Uncle Jack
 she'll grow up smart.
 He'll grow up smart
 he'll never pick apples."
I just talk away.
Emma holds my hand tighter,
offering me encouragement.
I don't care what the farmers think.
I hold Emma's hands and talk.
We both close our eyes,
and listen.

The perfect sky

I stop the car
a few kilometres from the farm,
at Broken Lookout.
Emma and I sit on the warm bonnet
and look at the distant farm lights.
We don't say much.
Birth classes take it all.
I tell Emma about my Mother.
Dead. Eight years now.
I tell her how I remember everything about her.
Her hair, her soft voice in the dark,
her way of looking at my sister and me.
I tell Emma I'll never forget a thing.
Not because my Mum's dead.
Not because I miss her.
But because she's my Mum
and it's important.
And before she died,
she taught me that.
She taught me what's important,
and what isn't.
And I've never forgotten.
And that's what mothers do, I say.
We look at the lights some more
under the perfect sky.
I try to remember every detail
of what's important.

Annabel and George

Jack and Emma were at birth classes last night.
I was in the shed, again.
Reading. Dreaming really,
of the beach,
of the world away from apples.
And George knocks at the door of his own shed.
He wants to talk.

He's worried Emma will leave, after the baby.
After we go.
She'll leave this farm, this land,
and him, and Craig, and Beck,
and home.
George is scared.
His voice is tight, his eyes darting.

I tell him to wait.
I tell him to look at Emma
and how she walks
and how she holds her stomach when she walks
as if she's protecting the child
as if she's afraid to let something precious fall.

I tell George to trust his daughter
and her hands.
I tell him those hands won't fail.
And I pray I'm right.

*A*nnabel

After George left
I couldn't read anymore.
I sat on the haybales
and tried to work things out.
But all I could think was that
I felt like an intruder,
here on the farm.
For weeks we'd been helpers.
When George couldn't get pickers,
we worked.
When Emma needed someone for classes,
we volunteered.
But now,
with George wandering his farm,
like a lost man,
waiting for Emma and Jack to come home,
I knew.
We were intruding.
It was all too private.
Maybe we were wrong,
wrong to offer with the classes,
I'm not sure.
Only now, maybe,
they needed each other,
not us.

Craig and his mad dad

I think Dad's going mad!
True.
Last night I saw him
wandering around the house
in his overalls and slippers.
It was a full moon
so I could see good
and you know what they say
about a full moon — it makes you mad!
Well, Dad's walking around the yard,
and he wanders out to the orchard.
He picks an apple,
a big juicy apple,
and I think,
fine, he's going to eat it.
But no.
He starts tossing it in the air,
higher and higher
and he catches it every time.
Now Dad hardly ever throws balls
and never but never throws apples.
He's always telling me
not to drop them into the bin
in case they bruise,
and here he is, a full moon,
playing catch with an apple.

Very weird.
He's out in the orchard forever it seems,
just walking around,
with this apple,
tossing it from one hand to the other.
And this is the best bit —
he walks back to the house
and he looks up
and sees me at the window.
I'm thinking I'm going to get it
for being up so late,
but all he does is cup his hands,
like this,
meaning he wants me to catch the apple.
So I lean right out the window
and Dad throws it, perfect!
I catch it with both hands.
I take a big crunchy bite
and Dad smiles
and waves goodnight.

It was a good apple too.
A good apple, picked by a madman,
on a full moon night.

Craig and cricket

At school today,
Sports Day,
we had our cricket final
against Blairthorn School.
Most of the school were there,
you know,
cheering us on.
I got out for a duck.
I lifted my head, as usual,
and got clean bowled.
But when Blairthorn were batting,
and it was getting tight,
their best batsmen
hit this huge shot
and it was going for four, or maybe six,
and I ran around the boundary,
dived full-length, sideways,
and caught it!
Everyone cheered,
and my duck was forgotten,
and now we stood a chance of winning.

It was a good catch,
my second good catch in 24 hours,
don't you reckon?

Emma and the right way

I've been thinking hard.
It's all I can do right now.
Think. And wait.

I needed Jack and Annabel
on this farm two months ago.
They came out of nowhere,
and gave me hope.
The way they were, together.
Everything they do is positive.
They're not like the kids at school.
I needed them.
I needed help with birth classes.
But now,
I've been thinking about Dad.
I've never thought about him.
He just was.
I worried about Mum, wherever she is.
I worried about Beck and Craig, without Mum.

But Dad, look at him.
Three children, no wife,
a farm that barely pays
and he gets up every morning
sits on the veranda
watching the sunrise

and he counts himself lucky.
And when I come home pregnant
he doesn't yell, or rant, or blame.
He just keeps on going.
He looks almost proud of me.
Now he worries I'll leave.
He worries Jack and Annabel leaving
will mean I'll follow,
maybe not after them, but away,
anywhere.
But he's not saying anything.
He's going to let me choose,
I know.
It's his way.
It's the right way.

*G*uts

Maybe I don't have the guts to leave.
It shouldn't be too hard.
Mum left.
She packed and was gone in a day.
Vanished.
I could do that,
only I'd write, and phone,
and maybe come back,
you know, later.
A girl, pregnant or not,
could get lost in the city.
And it couldn't be worse than here,
could it?
Bloody Mum. I hate her.
I hate her for going so easy.
For going and staying away.
Craig and Emma still hope she'll come back,
someday.

I can see it now.
I leave home
   for the city
   I'm walking down the street
   and guess who's walking towards me
   and what do I say to her
   "hello Mum"

or
   "hello Grandma."
Now that would be funny.
So funny I'd have to stop myself
from hitting her,
from telling her what I really think,
but maybe I don't have the guts
for that either.
But when I look at this farm
I keep thinking
it's not whether I have the guts to go
but
if I have the guts to stay.

*E*mma and leaving

Last night
Jack told me about the beach,
and his plans,
and the more he talked,
the more nervous I got.
I don't know why.
I can't tell.

I just listened.
I listened and dreamed.

And that's what I'm doing now.
I'm dreaming.
Only sometimes it's hard dreaming
when
Beck needs help with her homework
and Craig's talking nonstop
and Dad's burning the dinner
and my own kid's kicking his way around my belly.

So I'm not thinking good
when Beck,
bloody Beck,
she who never says a word,
looks up at me over the pages
and says

"you're smart,
you know that Emma?"

And it all makes sense,
even to smart old Emma.

A Young Orchard

A *young orchard*

It wasn't what Beck said,
but that she said it at all.
I knew.
I'm staying here.
No dreams of fancy clothes
    and cafes
    and movies
    and working in a sleek office tower.
It was old lino
and peeling paint
and apple pies every dessert
and my baby eating apple mush
and Craig and Beck and Dad.
But it was more than that,
it was me.
Me without Jack and Annabel
and some excuse to leave.
Me without Mum and the fear
of loneliness and boredom.
Me, making my way.
And Joseph, or Josephine.
Me, back at school.
Me, taking that bloody bus
    the twenty kilometres
    and the baby in childcare

while I study hard,
harder than ever before.
And me getting out of here,
my way,
when I'm ready,
with my child.
Me, getting out but
not like Mum,
running so fast
she's too scared to look back.
Me, getting out but
being able to come back.
Me and my home.
Me and the baby,
happy in the orchard
picking those stupid apples
if we choose.
Or me and my baby
leaving
finding another orchard
a young orchard
and making it ours.

nnabel

When we first came here
Jack and I had a picnic every Sunday.
We went to the channel
or across town to Brown Creek.
We lay on the blanket in the sun,
and slept. Or drank a few bottles,
and dived into the chill water.

Today we asked Emma along
and she said no.
She said no in a strange way,
and I think I know what she meant.

Here at Brown Creek
I lean over and pick up a few rocks.
I aim for a boulder on the far side of the creek.
I say to myself, as Jack sleeps,
if the first one hits
we leave this week
and drive, non-stop, to the beach.

I choose the biggest rock
and let rip,
and my aim is true.

*N*ow

Jack wakes,
and I tell him of the boulder
and my perfect aim.

I tell him I've decided,
we leave this week.
We fill the car with petrol now,
just to be sure.

I tell him I'm not angry,
or crazy.
I tell him I'm ready,
and he should be too.
I tell him to think of our two years together.
Think of us leaving Uni and ending up here.
Think of us making love on a stack of haybales.
Think of the mornings in the orchard
and the taste of dew-fresh apples.
Think of him and me and Emma at birth classes.
Think of Craig and his painted cows.
Think of Emma here on the farm
and the rich soil of family.

And it makes sense, I know.
I hit the boulder with one throw,
and it made a strong ringing sound,
that echoed back across the creek.
We're leaving.

Emma and her Dad

Jack and Annabel
have filled their car with petrol, at last,
and gone on a Sunday drive.
A picnic, like young lovers.
They asked me along.
I said no.
I said, stay young lovers together,
and they looked at me funny.

Dad's working on the tractor, again.
Beck and Craig are in the treehouse,
playing quiet, for a change.
I take Dad some tea,
and this cake I made,
which wouldn't win any prizes
but it's OK —
I don't want to be a cook or anything.

Me and Dad sit by the tractor,
the dogs hang around for food
and the afternoon settles
on an orchard stripped of fruit.
The season is over.
Jack and Annabel can go whenever they like.
They've been waiting,
the whole farm's been waiting,
waiting for me to have this baby.

I start talking to Dad
about my baby
about Mum leaving us
and never coming back.
I tell him about school
and the long afternoons in Maths
when I dreamed myself away,
away anywhere.
And about Jack and Annabel,
smart and ready
and I'm wondering where all that smart comes from
and I figure some from parents,
some from school, and some from a place inside you.
I tell Dad
I got smart from him,
and I'm smart deep inside,
but from school I got nothing but pregnant.

I can curse school for that or curse myself,
but what's the point.
So I think school deserves more
and I say to Dad
I want to go back to school
after the baby
and for the first time in a while
Dad looks straight at me

and I'm scared to look back
because I'm not sure what it means
so I keep talking.
I tell him I rang Childcare in town
and I rang the Department
and I know it'll be hard
but it won't cost much
for the baby to be looked after
while I'm in school
and I know I can manage it
maybe even Beck and Craig can help.
I know I can do it
and I keep talking
afraid to look at Dad
and I say
Jack and Annabel should go,
go to their beach,
before the baby, who's taking his own good time.
I'll tell them thanks
and I'll promise an invitation
to the Christening.
I look straight at Dad now
knowing I have to
and he's still looking back.
I tell him when Jack goes

I'll need help with birth classes
and maybe he could come along
and he smiles.
I think it's a Dad smile.
He leans over
and takes another slice of cake
and he keeps smiling
and he says,
calm as you please
"You make a good cake Emma
  a good cake"
and I know everything will be fine,
just fine.
So I reach for a slice
to feed my baby
and myself.
I take a big slice.

A Full Tank

Craig knows

Me and Beck,
we're gunna miss you two.
We reckon you're lucky,
leaving here to spend all your time
on some beach.
Maybe we can visit
on school holidays or something?
You let us know OK?

I'm gunna miss you two.
I like the way you get drunk
every Saturday night
when you think the farm's asleep.
I like the way
you sleep late on Sunday
and stumble out of the shed
like two old drunks.
But most of all I like
the way you spend your nights
up there, on the haybales.

Yeah, that's right,
one night I couldn't sleep
and I came out here, real quiet,
so yeah,
now I know what you do in our shed!

*I*t's time

We've packed the car,
Annabel and me.
I've filled the tank with petrol,
this time, we won't stop.

I wander into the orchard, alone.
I'm looking for the first tree I stripped,
two months back.
I'm sure I'll remember which one.
It was on the end of a line,
the highest on the farm.
The view looked over the valley and the hills,
and all the way to Broken Lookout.
I climb the tree,
and sit for a while.
The rotting fruit covers the grass
and the leaves are starting to drop.
I hear a crow up in the fir trees,
and a semitrailer on the distant highway.
And I can hear my Dad's voice
telling me to go, just go.

I hear Annabel's footsteps,
coming through the grove
and I know
that my world echoes with her sound

and that I should follow it,
the way Emma will follow her baby,
hopeful, and sure,
and tied to this farm
and these people.
I know
that today,
with a full tank,
and with Annabel,
that it's time to go.

Annabel and the orchard

Jack's up some tree.
Dreaming.
I hope the branch breaks
and he lands on his head.
That's how I feel sometimes.
But I'm glad we argued over leaving.
Sometimes you need to make a choice.
Like giving up Uni.
Like coming to this farm to work.
Like Emma getting drunk one night,
waking up pregnant,
and still saying yes to the baby
after all that.
Like me and Jack now, together,
going.
Starting now.
Starting today.
When we leave this orchard.
That is, if I can get my love, the mad bastard,
out of the tree.

Warm

*F*or the sun

It's the first rain of the season.
I think of Jack and Annabel
on some beach. I hope the sun shines there.
I can hear Dad chopping wood,
ready for a long cold spell
with frost on the orchard
cracking under our feet.
The clouds have covered the hills
and the trees are stark winter bones.
I touch my stomach, gently,
feel such power and weight
but if I get any bigger
they'll need a wheelbarrow
to get me to hospital.
I love my baby.
I don't care how it happened.
I don't care how cold this winter gets.
I stand on the veranda
and feel warmer than I've ever felt.
The wind rattles the shed door
to remind me of Jack and Annabel.
I hope they're swimming naked
in clear salty water.
I'm glad they came.
I can see Craig and Beck
walking home from the highway.

Craig's swinging his lunatic school-bag
and Beck's wandering slow, in no hurry.
I sit on the squatter's chair
put my feet up on the veranda railing,
lean back, close my eyes,
and wait, for the sun.

Look for *Love, Ghosts, & Facial Hair*, the companion novel to *A Place Like This*.

I'm a normal guy.

An average sixteen-year-old.

I think about sex, sport, & nose hair.

Sex mostly.

Jack's got a lot on his mind: He's trying to figure out the mystery of the opposite sex, he can't stop wondering about facial hair, and he won't let go of his mother's ghost, even though she died seven years ago. Jack knows he can't hang on to the past forever, but what he doesn't know is how to let go.

Then he meets Annabel. She's beautiful, smart, and she *gets* him. Suddenly love makes sense, and the future seems hopeful. And for the first time, Jack feels ready to leave the past where it belongs.

Available from Simon Pulse